Praise for *Lean Sigma—Rebuilding Capability in Healthcare*

"Ian has been a valued business partner for many years. His most recent focus in our strategic planning process has been extremely helpful to us as we develop our vision, plan, and deployment map for the next several years. His expertise, discipline, and approaches are excellent."

—*Jim Bickel, President and CEO at Columbus Regional Hospital*

"The Affordable Care Act (ACA) looks like it is around to stay. It will require hospitals and other healthcare organizations to become ruthlessly efficient to survive reimbursement rate reductions. Even if ACA fell, managed care organizations have caught on. They will leverage patient volume to drive reimbursement rates steadily down. Medicare and Medicaid will follow. Lean Sigma may not be the only way healthcare organizations will survive, but it's a proven solution. In *Lean Sigma—Rebuilding Capability in Healthcare*, Dr. Wedgwood has presented a roadmap to successful implementation of Lean Sigma."

—*Richard H. Allen, Dr.P.H., Allen & Allen Consulting, LLC*

Lean Sigma

REBUILDING CAPABILITY IN HEALTHCARE

Lean Sigma

REBUILDING CAPABILITY
IN HEALTHCARE

Ian Wedgwood, Ph.D.

PRENTICE
HALL

Upper Saddle River, NJ • Boston • Indianapolis • San Francisco
New York • Toronto • Montreal • London • Munich • Paris • Madrid
Capetown • Sydney • Tokyo • Singapore • Mexico City

Many of the designations used by manufacturers and sellers to distinguish their products are claimed as trademarks. Where those designations appear in this book, and the publisher was aware of a trademark claim, the designations have been printed with initial capital letters or in all capitals.

The author and publisher have taken care in the preparation of this book, but make no expressed or implied warranty of any kind and assume no responsibility for errors or omissions. No liability is assumed for incidental or consequential damages in connection with or arising out of the use of the information or programs contained herein.

For information about buying this title in bulk quantities, or for special sales opportunities (which may include electronic versions; custom cover designs; and content particular to your business, training goals, marketing focus, or branding interests), please contact our corporate sales department at corpsales@pearsoned.com or (800) 382-3419.

For government sales inquiries, please contact governmentsales@pearsoned.com.

For questions about sales outside the United States, please contact international@pearsoned.com.

Visit us on the Web: informit.com/ph

Library of Congress Cataloging-in-Publication Data
Wedgwood, Ian, author.
  [Lean sigma (2015)]
  Lean sigma : rebuilding capability in healthcare / Ian Wedgwood.
       p.   ; cm.
  Includes bibliographical references and index.
  ISBN 978-0-13-399200-7 (pbk. : alk. paper)—ISBN 0-13-399200-4 (pbk. : alk. paper)
  I. Title
  [DNLM: 1. Quality of Health Care—organization & administration.
2. Efficiency, Organizational. 3. Organizational Case Studies. 4. Organizational Innovation. 5. Quality Assurance, Health Care—methods.   W. 84.41]
  R728
  362.1068—dc23
                                                            2014049451

AIDET® is a registered trademark of The Studer Group, LLC.

Figures 4.2 and 4.3 are used with permission from Columbus Regional Health.

ISBN-13: 978-0-13-399200-7
ISBN-10: 0-13-399200-4
Text printed in the United States on recycled paper at Courier in Westford, Massachusetts.
First printing, March 2015

Executive Editor
Bernard Goodwin

Editor
Chris Guzikowski

Managing Editor
John Fuller

Senior Production Editor
Mary Kesel Wilson

Copy Editor
Barbara Wood

Indexer
Jack Lewis

Proofreader
Linda Begley

Editorial Assistant
Michelle Housley

Cover Designer
Alan Clements

Compositor
Shepherd, Inc.

This book is dedicated to my son Sean, who inspires me daily to work to make healthcare better and safer for those we hold dearest.

Contents

PREFACE

OVERVIEW

Healthcare over the past decade has been required to undergo significant fundamental change—change that will likely continue for the foreseeable future. Most healthcare organizations have risen to the challenge, yet many are struggling to achieve the desired success. The intent of this book is not to examine the external factors driving these changes; there are many other texts dedicated to that particular task.[1] Rather, the focus here is on examining the internal factors causing the struggles: the organizational capabilities of structuring and executing change through performance improvement methodologies—specifically, one of the more successful ones, Lean Sigma.

Lean and Six Sigma are well-understood change concepts outside healthcare. With well over 20 years of success in multiple industries, the results speak for themselves. Major corporations show savings in annual reports measured in hundreds of millions of dollars and even billions of dollars. Finally the push is being made into healthcare. Unfortunately, as Lean Sigma makes headway in healthcare, there seem to be so many misconceptions about what it really is—for example, that it is merely a toolkit akin to existing improvement methods.

---

1. One such example is *Escape Fire*, by Donald M. Berwick. Also, the Commonwealth Fund releases regular updates on the state of healthcare in the United States relative to other countries in its *Mirror, Mirror* report.

These many misconceptions present problems in that they remove many of the key facets that make Lean Sigma different, the same ones that in practice make it work successfully.

The intent here is to explain how the Lean Sigma approach, so successful in other industries, can be readily transferred to healthcare and give comparable, if not greater, results.

This book is in no way meant to be a technical text. Most guides at this point switch to "stat speak" and both confuse and alienate the reader with technical jargon. This is not the essence of Lean Sigma. Lean Sigma is not rocket science. Practitioners of Lean Sigma don't need a deep technical or statistics background. Experience shows that often the best practitioners do *not* have a statistics background at all.

The book is predominantly about change and how to manage it at an organizational level. Lean Sigma is a change initiative. It is designed as a means to improve a business. Any business. It draws from the successes of previous initiatives and adds critical elements where previous initiatives failed. In simple terms, Lean Sigma is a business performance improvement methodology that

- Focuses on processes
- Aims to find root causes versus merely tackling symptoms
- Makes change via well-scoped projects
- Ensures that projects are the right projects by linking them directly to the business goals
- Ensures that the right resources are involved at all levels
- Ensures that barriers are identified and removed
- Carefully tracks progress to ensure success
- Utilizes individuals drawn from the organization to become a pool of well-trained change resources to lead projects
- Utilizes consistent, well-defined roadmaps to solve process problems using data, not speculation or gut feel
- Ensures that robust controls are in place to sustain any gains

This list makes absolute sense—nothing in this book should seem to be more than common sense. There are no smoke and mirrors involved—in fact no magic at all. This is just a robust method for making business performance improvement.

So why then do so many in healthcare falter when they come to apply such a commonsense approach? Unfortunately there are multiple reasons for this.

- It does require an investment of leadership, which often goes unrecognized.
- It doesn't fit the existing change model, and leaders don't know how to integrate it into their business.
- Practitioners of existing (typically quality) approaches, both inside the organization as well as external consultants, try to position this as something they were already doing and thus never really progress.
- It is perceived as an extension of existing methods and therefore does not get the appropriate attention and effort.
- Purveyors of Lean Sigma training often just focus on the simpler and more lucrative mass training of staff, instead of the critical but more difficult in-depth leadership training and guidance.
- There is a misconception around just how many change resources are required to make the difference that is being sought ("All we need is one Black Belt and off we go").
- Change is difficult in the best of cases, but it has been too easy to say, "We're different from other industries, so it won't work here."
- Key stakeholders take the stance that because of its industrial roots, Lean Sigma doesn't apply to healthcare; this drives a desire to blindly tailor and diminish the approach without first understanding the full context and facets.
- Healthcare is an industry that thrives on quick solutions. The desire to take shortcuts brings about a dumbing down of sophisticated approaches to the point that they are no better than existing methods, which is then followed by asking the bizarre question, "Why is this any different?"
- Leaders and managers are scared of airing dirty laundry in the more open environment of a Lean Sigma culture.

And last, but arguably most important,

- There is often a firmly held belief that the route to improvement in healthcare is through its people, not its processes, and hence the broken, disconnected, or disjointed processes are never addressed.

Many of these arguments relate to healthcare being positioned as different from other industries. Typical phrases are "We're not a factory or an assembly line" or just simply "We're different; that won't work here." It is correct to state that healthcare is different from any other industry, but to be frank, it's different in all the same ways. Hospitals, health systems, and their staff

- Interact with customers (patients and physicians)
- Use established processes to perform their work (clinical guidelines, best practices, etc.)
- Are supplied with "stuff" (materials, equipment, and supplies)
- Deliver value in the form of services (assessments, treatments, etc.) and goods (implants, bandages, etc.)
- Invoice customers for the value provided to them
- Collect monetary return for services rendered
- Rely on financial performance as well as quality and associated customer satisfaction

Viewing healthcare in this context, Lean Sigma is absolutely transferable to and wholly applicable in healthcare.[2]

Who This Book Is For

This is a guide for everyone in the healthcare industry (from clinics to hospitals to health systems), from the sharp-end, patient-facing staff to the senior executives. It should be applicable to physicians, nurses, staff, executives, administrators, and quality and compliance groups alike. It is meant for those seeking to understand how to bring an effective Lean Sigma program to their organization, or to better their current program.

This is not a guide for an untrained project leader—don't expect to read this and be able to lead a Lean Sigma project (this book will just make you dangerous). However, for the trained Belt, Chapter 3 may open your eyes to a new way of thinking about your work.

Neither is this book intended to teach the reader how to use the tools associated with Lean Sigma. There are other texts that provide that instruction,

---

2. For concrete examples and success stories, see Chapter 4.

including the author's.[3] This book will explore the infrastructure necessary and sequencing of Lean Sigma projects and why they are important, not tool execution. This text and books on tool instruction are useful companions to each other.

The conclusions in this book are based on the author's two decades of experience in deploying Lean Sigma, leading projects, and consulting across multiple industries, with more than a decade of that time in healthcare. None of this is theory or conjecture, so it should appeal to the practitioner—the practical, and the pragmatic alike.

How to Use the Book

The book is meant to be read end to end. The goal is to broaden the readers' thinking and expose them to facets of change that are not normally considered. It is probably unwise to skip sections. There is much misunderstanding of Lean Sigma in healthcare, which is probably in part a result of making assumptions to fill gaps in the fabric of understanding. Read the whole text to understand the framework—don't just pick and choose.

This book centers on the leadership aspects of a change program and is structured as follows:

- Chapter 1 highlights the failure points in the existing change methods and how they contrive to prevent healthcare performance from truly improving.
- Chapter 2 explains the structured change approach of Lean Sigma at a program level, across projects: how it fits with strategy, operations, and other initiatives.
- Chapter 3 gives a high-level overview within a project of the roadmap and tools—that is, how to tackle an individual process and elevate its performance level.
- Chapter 4 gives case study examples of the application of Lean Sigma to different areas in various healthcare organizations: the focus, approaches, achievements, and leadership learning.
- Chapter 5 explains the various stages of maturity of a program and how best to start to bring this to your organization.

---

3. Ian Wedgwood, *Lean Sigma: A Practitioner's Guide* (Prentice Hall, 2006).

The book can be used as a tool to support commencement or reinvigoration of a deployment of Lean Sigma across an organization, so once you've read it

- Hand it to (other) senior executive team members.
- Distribute it to all leaders and managers.
- Use it as a communication tool: "Read this, then we'll talk."

ACKNOWLEDGMENTS

I'd like to acknowledge the host of healthcare leaders across dozens of client organizations who helped shape the understanding and viewpoints shared in this book.

A special thank you to Jim Bickel, CEO, and his team at Columbus Regional Health (CRH), and in particular to Marlene Weatherwax, CFO, and Doug Sabotin, Director of Lean Sigma. I'd also like to thank the project and department leaders who provided the case examples in Chapter 4, including Carolyn O'Neal, Sharon Chandler, Natalie Thieret, and Bill Algee at CRH; Nikki Tumey and Bob Siegmann at Centerstone Behavioral Health; Kevin Knoll at Floyd Memorial Health; and Debbie Hudson at Norton Health.

Thanks also to Dr. Richard Allen for his supporting insight and work to review the manuscript, despite my congenital aversion to commas.

As always, I just don't have enough words to express my appreciation to my wife, Veronica, and my sons, Christian and Sean, who encourage and support me in everything I do.

Finally, to all the performance improvement and quality groups working tirelessly every day to make healthcare safer for us all: to you we are all indebted.

About the Author

Dr. Ian Wedgwood, President and CEO of Haelan Group, has more than 20 years of experience guiding organizations through change. He has led and facilitated dozens of Lean Sigma deployments in industries as diverse as healthcare, electronics, engineered materials, chemicals, banking, and hospitality, and has trained and mentored numerous executives, Champions, and Belts.

Ian's healthcare focus for the past decade has been guiding leadership in organizations ranging from large systems to single hospitals, from behavioral health to managed care.

He holds a Ph.D. and First-Class Honors degree in Applied Mathematics from Scotland's St. Andrew's University. He authored *Lean Sigma: A Practitioner's Guide,* considered a seminal work in the field of Lean, Six Sigma, and performance improvement.

EXISTING 1 CHANGE MODELS

Why the Traditional Healthcare Models Are Struggling

TRADITIONAL CHANGE MODELS

As described in the Preface, the general consensus is that performance (and performance improvement for that matter) in healthcare is not where it needs to be. Numerous articles and publications each year identify the problems or argue the root cause. The intent here is not to delve too deeply into the argument, but to highlight one key problem (in this case with the performance improvement methods utilized) and then, in the chapters to come, to demonstrate a solid solution to that problem. Consider the following symptoms:

- There is a sense of resource overloading—it is difficult to get team time to even start a project.
- Most improvement is incremental; there is little in the way of breakthrough change.
- Hard savings are just that: hard to come by and even harder to measure.

- It is difficult to attribute any measured success to specific changes made.
- Improvements fail to stick.

Not all organizations exhibit all these symptoms, but they are certainly commonplace, whether in a small clinic, a hospital, or a system. So if the symptoms are clear and abundant, why, with all the effort under way, are the symptoms still the norm?

The usual approach is to critique the solutions implemented and work from there. Here the suggestion is to look at things in a different way. The place to look is not at the solutions implemented, but rather at the improvement methodologies used—the *route* to solution and implementation.

To better understand this statement, first let's examine facets of the traditional improvement methods. Improvement is often undertaken as follows:

- Multiple groups are sanctioned (often independently) to make improvements, to bring agile responsive change.
- Operations and clinical managers are measured on the improvements they make.
- All quality and operations staff in the process are encouraged to make changes and test improvements, to develop change quickly, and to rapidly take advantage of potential improvements.
- Small group efforts are focused on a localized part of the process to alleviate the problem, and then the group moves on to the next focus area.
- Changes made require a consensus of as many stakeholders as possible to ensure buy-in from the people who will do the new process or be affected by it.
- A key source of improvements is from benchmarking other organizations, typically in relatively close proximity or from recent literature, to gain quick, proven solutions.
- The change model is based on continuous improvement using a cyclical PDCA[1] (Plan, Do, Check, Act) change model—looping through the cycle again and again to gain higher and higher levels of performance.
- Stand-alone quality groups own process improvement in the organization, so that operational staff aren't drawn away from their operations duties.
- The focus is on getting better leaders, managers, and communication by developing the existing people or recruiting better people.

---

1. Sometimes referred to as the PDSA (Plan, Do, Study, Act) model, or the "The Scientific Method."

At first glance this seems to be a robust set of operating approaches for change, which accounts for their longevity in the healthcare industry. Why, then, do the majority of other industries and organizations not use these approaches? They do seem reasonable—until, that is, we start to line up the symptoms with the change model, and then the flaws become very apparent. This is best shown through an example, as follows. Consider a scenario of operations or clinical managers trying to meet assigned targets, perhaps to increase patient satisfaction by 10% or similar. They do what they've been trained to do: they talk to as many people as possible to find a solution that seems to work well in another hospital or institution; on returning to home base they bring together as many people in the process as possible to gain some kind of consensus; they educate key personnel on the solution and commence operations with the new method; they then track the metric (in this case patient satisfaction) to see what, if any, change has occurred.

Oftentimes the metric will improve, but sometimes not, and commonly over time it drops back to where it was before. Sometimes it even gets worse than it was when the change initiative started.

Meanwhile, others in the organization are going through the same motions for the same process (usually under the direction of a different change group). They, too, are finding the "best solution" and bringing it back home, training a few people, and measuring impacts.

Over time, change is continuously occurring, but performance improvement doesn't necessarily follow.

The problems here are actually quite simple to categorize, and we'll examine each in more detail in the remainder of this chapter:

- There are disparate change groups.
- There is uncontained change.
- There is no standard change approach.
- The belief is that simple tools can fix the problems.
- There is a reliance on benchmarking to provide the solutions.
- Changes are not made based on data, or on the right data.
- Changes are made based on symptoms, not causes.
- Focus is on systems rather than processes.
- Focus is on people, not on processes.
- There is a lack of context for solutions, and in particular an unclear understanding of the Voice of the Customer (VOC).

- Solutions involve adding extra activities to the process (patching) instead of subtracting activities from the process (streamlining).
- Implementation is poor and limited in magnitude.
- There is little or no emphasis on sustaining the improved process, or control.
- There is confusion regarding the roles of management versus leadership.

To an objective observer, some of these issues are readily apparent. To those in the heat of battle of patient care, they are considered part of everyday life, are accepted norms, and are overlooked or aren't perceived as the key issues to be addressed.

Let's take a look at each in turn and how they can combine to have such a negative impact on future performance.

DISPARATE CHANGE GROUPS

In most hospitals there are multiple change groups and modes in operation, to name a few: local management-sanctioned change, clinical quality groups, nursing leadership, compliance groups, operations groups, senior executives, medical quality groups, and so on.

Each team formed is typically woefully underresourced and must fight to get meeting time (and often space), and often multiple teams are focused on resolving problems in the same target process. Project 1 can't get team time because another team meeting for Project 2 involving the same people is meeting at the same time (sometimes even related to the same process issues).

Quality improvement (typically limited to clinical quality) is managed separately from operational improvement. The quality organization is usually a disconnected silo, too often focused primarily on regulatory compliance, and often plays second fiddle to any operations group. Many a quality group has asked how they might get support from operations when they want to run a project. Surely this is the tail trying to wag the dog. Would it not be more appropriate for the operations group to be frequently approaching the quality group in search of the skills and resources for operational improvement projects?

Quality groups instead spend valuable time canvassing to get the right people in the room and aren't empowered to recruit the organizational manpower they need. Oftentimes they just shy away from the difficulty of getting an individual in the room at all and resort to "cubicle projects."[2]

---

2. Where the project is progressed essentially in a vacuum in a quality group member's cubicle.

Even in operations the functions are siloed, and broad-scoped, cross-functional change is difficult to come by. Take, for example, a typical emergency department, where ED staff function almost entirely independently of the registration staff working side by side in the same process. Due to this siloing of functions, operations, and change groups, change is made in a nonunified way and breakthrough changes (usually found in aligning the handoffs from function to function) are rare.

UNCONTAINED CHANGE

When change is made by so many disparate groups, it occurs in a nonuniform, uncontained, and often poorly understood way. Change is unmanaged, with one change overlapping the next, and the process is never allowed to settle. Deming[3] gave a wonderful demonstration of rolling a marble around a funnel to hit a spot on the floor. By consciously trying to manipulate the dropping process to improve it, an operator only makes things worse (the operator is in fact merely adding variability to the process). It is not until the operator lets the process settle, and doesn't add change after change after change, that the process begins to perform consistently and in fact better.

If a process is constantly in flux, it is virtually impossible to get a pulse on how well it truly can perform, since any snapshot in time is essentially of a different process. Also, as performance does improve, it is very difficult, if not impossible, to understand which change the performance improvement can be attributed to and hence which changes to keep.

The greatest problem with uncontained change then occurs: a potentially well-performing process is overwritten with a poorer one. Uncontained change leads to no standardization or consistency across units or shifts or even individuals on the same shift, and the process literally just keeps changing and changing and often never truly improves. This phenomenon, aptly named "1-sigma churn,"[4] is absolutely the norm across hospitals.

---

3. Dr. William Edwards Deming (1900–1993) was an American engineer, statistician, professor, author, lecturer, and management consultant and is considered to be one of the founders of business performance improvement.

4. A term coined by Tim Tarnowski (at the time of writing with Indiana University Health) early in the Lean Sigma deployment at Columbus Regional Hospital.

NO STANDARD CHANGE APPROACH

Disparate improvement groups typically use different approaches to making performance improvement. There is a difference between groups, but there is also a difference within the groups and often even an individual will use different approaches at different times. The driver for this is that there is almost always a clear understanding of the need for standards set around operations, but that same level of understanding doesn't extend to the need for setting accountability to follow a standard approach or roadmap in making change.

The problems this causes are multifold. It leads to inconsistent and therefore unpredictable timelines. Projects often start slowly with reasonable discipline but then have to accelerate when organizational patience runs out. Acceleration is synonymous with cutting corners and making decisions based on gut feel. Change agents have to "give their best shot," and decisions are assumptions at best. Also, due to the unpredictability in timelines, it is very difficult to predict future resource requirements, which leads inevitably to all kinds of project resource clashes later. It also makes it very difficult to understand the current status of projects, and without a good yardstick for progress, activity tends to just drag on. The statement "A conclusion is where people [the organization] got tired of thinking" is highly appropriate here.

The differences in approach can also cause frustration in individuals and between groups. Change Agent A is held to performing with a higher level of rigor and chided for not making progress quickly enough, whereas Agent B isn't fettered with the same approach and brings change (not necessarily the right change, but change nonetheless) more quickly and is aptly rewarded. This quickly drives an "us versus them" mentality between groups. The problem is exacerbated when trying to resource projects. The more disciplined group may find it difficult to get project teams together since their approach perhaps isn't as exciting or just takes too long. People in general seem to prefer the adrenaline rush of "shooting from the hip" to the grind of working through the details. Subsequently there is erosion over time of the disciplined approach and its credibility, which likely will have a larger and insidious negative impact on the organization than just failed individual changes.

TOOLS FOCUS

The majority of people making changes in hospitals have never been formally trained in any improvement methods beyond rudimentary techniques. Complex change management requires something more than a flowchart or a quick team decision to resolve.

The ad hoc use of simple tools in projects is clearly better than using no tools at all. However, the approach misses two critical aspects of performance improvement. First, using tools independently without a systematic roadmap fails to illuminate the linkage between tools so that they build upon one another and advance critical thinking. Second, it fails to recognize the importance of an organizational infrastructure necessary at a program level to prioritize, align, and appropriately resource change.

By hiding behind the tools, change agents revert to the cubicle change model mentioned earlier. There is an unwillingness and inability to challenge the more difficult issues, which are often the more important ones in the organization. When the infrastructure elements are not considered, change groups are disconnected from the strategic direction of the organization, and there is no real understanding of what's really motivating leadership.

With this low-level thinking, change managers are not considered in a professional role. Projects are handed to untrained, inexperienced project leaders who, with no data-driven, systematic approaches available to them, in effect do little more than "wing it."

Even when more advanced infrastructure-based change methodologies, such as Lean Sigma, come along, the thinking is more about just adding a few more tools to the toolkit versus truly embracing a more advanced, higher-performing model; the effect is essentially to neuter the methodology in the process.

RELIANCE ON BENCHMARKING

Very few processes anywhere in healthcare are good from end to end. Admittedly there are pockets of good performance out there, but under scrutiny it's generally found that the performance is due to the *people* involved, not the robustness, reliability, and clarity of the process. High performance is related to high-performing teams working extremely hard to maintain it. These teams often exhibit high stress, burnout, and high turnover. Once the team lead goes home or, worse still, leaves the organization, performance quickly returns to typical levels. Let's face it—we're working hard, not smart.

And yet, unbelievable as it may seem, healthcare organizations still choose to use the copycat approach as their most important concept ideation tool.

Benchmarking is seen as a solution to problems, and yet the benchmarking undertaken is often without the context of understanding the existing process, its customers, and its suppliers. It is also not often done with the depth of under-standing required of the "better" process. This process may in effect be serving a different market, with a different volume and mix of patients, organizational setup, staff, and physicians, and yet it is lifted and copied as is (in a complete unit) to replace an existing process, which sometimes is better.

For some, a full-time role is to benchmark others and find "best practice." The overlooked flaw here is that what might be best practice for others may not be for us. What is deemed an evidence-based answer is just that, *an* answer. The problem is that it might not be an answer to *our* question.

For some, the primary focus is to be a benchmarked organization. In the modern healthcare market it is in fact beneficial to be *seen* to be successful, which yet further propagates this activity. Whole conferences (very large ones at that) are set up to encourage sharing and testing others' processes. As one patient I spoke with so succinctly put it, "Fine, but don't test it out on me!"

For some reason this seems to be a particularly difficult truth to accept. In one prestigious health system I visited, a quality leader threw her hands in the air in exasperation and surprise that benchmarking isn't the primary solution generator in more advanced change methodologies such as Lean Sigma.

This steadfast belief in the grass being greener on the other side of the street further drives the 1-sigma churn. For every new benchmarking conference, staff members bring back someone else's process, overwriting again and again their own process without context or control.

CHANGES ARE NOT BASED ON DATA, GOOD DATA, OR THE RIGHT DATA

When first starting in process improvement in healthcare, one is generally and genuinely surprised at the sheer volume of data available, much more so than in any other industry. On closer scrutiny, though, it becomes apparent that the data and related measurement systems are invalid or unreliable. For example, it is commonplace for emergency departments to measure length of stay (LOS) for patients. In practice, the LOS data collected represents only a fraction of the true duration from when patients arrive at the hospital site to when they leave (typi-cally the captured measure runs only from registration to disposition). Simi-larly, when asked to provide data for leadership presentations, analysts often ask, "What do you want it to show?" In a recent surgery project, patient data was stored in 16 (*sixteen*) databases, none of which were in sync.

There is a lot of data, but not much valuable information.

With poor measurement systems and the resultant data they produce, it becomes very difficult to understand with any real confidence what drives process performance and subsequently what could make breakthrough change. With little in the way of supporting evidence, managers often believe they have to be the ones to come up with all the solutions, and usually no one will challenge them. Even if they were to make decisions based on the data available, the statistical validity would be questionable.

Simple Measurement Systems Analysis (MSA) studies on data systems thought to be robust quickly show a different picture. For example, in one hospital's analysis of the charge capture and subsequent coding of cath lab procedures, it was discovered that coders were all in complete agreement with each other less than 10% of the time and even with themselves only 60% of the time.

Even when improvements are made, without good measurement systems (and therefore data) any change in performance is difficult to detect (due to being shrouded in measurement system noise), reliably verify, or attribute to the changes made.

Quite often it's just the wrong data or the wrong focus. We're simply asking the wrong question. A useful example here is one of a project leader trying to improve the access for pregnant women to prenatal education. By asking a number of times in succession, "Why do we care?" the true underlying problem is revealed.[5] Mothers need better access to education prior to the delivery visit. Why do we care? Because if they are educated during delivery, they tend to forget things in the stressful environment and retention is not good. Why do we care? Because mothers need to be educated in how to care for themselves and their newborn. Why do we care? Because, after they leave the hospital, informed mothers can successfully prevent complications and avoid an unnecessary return. By digging in this way, the project leader recognized that the real goal (and hence the data required) related to the reduction in the number of unnecessary postnatal readmissions. By focusing on this as the needed data, the team managed to improve how the education was delivered and what was delivered as well as improve access to the education to ensure the best retention and subsequent care.

---

5. Described in Ian Wedgwood, *Lean Sigma: A Practitioner's Guide* (Prentice Hall, 2006), Chapter 7.01, pp. 120–21.

CHANGES MADE BASED ON SYMPTOMS, NOT CAUSES

The majority of metrics in healthcare are lagging indicators of performance, merely symptoms of the process versus true process metrics closely tied to the real-time performance of the process—for example, mortality, morbidity, ventilator-associated pneumonia or VAP rates, falls, and employee engagement. Many metrics are composite metrics, made up of many drivers—for example, patient satisfaction and physician satisfaction.

When improvement (or decline) occurs in lagging or composite metrics, it's very difficult, sometimes impossible, to relate it back to any changes made.

Finally, lagging data captured in the process is often used as a control for ensuring that the process consistently meets performance requirements. Such metrics are almost useless as control metrics, being captured monthly or even quarterly or annually when context is not available and not much could be done to react even if the cause were known. When trying to drive improvement in processes, if the measures used are just symptoms and not real process metrics, it's just a matter of "track and hope" at best.

SYSTEMS VERSUS PROCESSES

As in many other industries, staff in healthcare struggle with the differentiation between systems and processes. In simple terms, processes are "*what*" is (supposed to be) happening and "*how*" it occurs; systems are the things that support processes. For example, take a materials tracking system in a surgery (say). The process is made up of the steps, triggers, roles, responsibilities, and skills to ensure that material physically moves from the dock through the hospital to the operating room and beyond. The system involved merely tracks what's occurring in support of the process to ensure that the current state is reflected and understood at all times (as shown in Figure 1.1).

When material is unavailable, it is therefore inappropriate to blame the system when what has truly failed is the process. Also, it is naïve to believe that "all these problems will be resolved when we install xyz system or upgrade to version x.x of the software." The impact of this has been a painful lesson for a great many organizations that implemented an electronic medical records (EMR) system in the past few years. Likewise, it is misguided to believe that a systems-based approach to performance improvement will change the physical aspects of the organization's processes. Such an approach tries to tackle certain

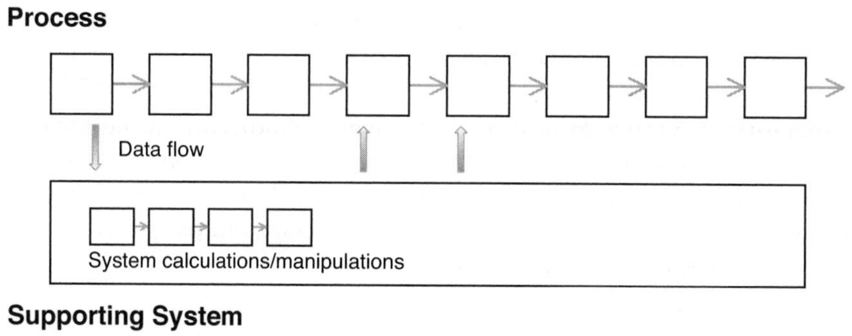

Process

Supporting System

Figure 1.1 The relationship between process and system

symptoms house-wide all at the same time, when the needs, context, and organizational setup are different from process to process. An example might be the desire to improve communication (say). True, communication is important in many instances, but without a detailed understanding of the requirements of a particular trigger, the communication mechanism imposed may not be the best (or required at all).

FOCUS ON PEOPLE, NOT ON PROCESS

Similar to systems thinking, there is also a tendency to think that solutions will be found in the people, not the process. A number of approaches from improvement to communications methods, teaming, leadership, people management, time management, and so on are undertaken with the naïve hope that these will change the fundamental physics of the process. Not surprisingly, without changing the processes, everything from a performance perspective effectively remains the same, barring minor short-lived incremental improvement. With no significant shift in performance, leadership over the process is often replaced (remember, the focus is on people versus the process), and the next installed leader adds his or her patches and tweaks (propagating the 1-sigma churn). This revolving-door practice is very common in the higher-stress areas of hospitals, particularly in surgical services and emergency departments. The churn is broken only when a leader has the insight or foresight to take apart the process.

This is not to say that people aren't important in process improvement, but as will be described in Chapter 2, the initial focus should be on the physics and engineering of the process: the mechanics, activities, layout, triggers, flow, roles, accountabilities, and metrics. The softer elements of communication, teaming, and leadership will come into play once the fundamentals are in place. In effect, by focusing on the people first, we're "coming in from the wrong end."

Let's imagine taking the people to one side. The process is what remains. If it is missing, disconnected, broken, misaligned, or flawed in any way, when we layer our people back onto it, we frustrate them and they have to become inventive to work around the process. Our most valued asset, our people, is successful *despite* our processes, not because of them.[6]

LACK OF CONTEXT FOR SOLUTIONS

As described in the previous "Disparate Change Groups" discussion, it is often difficult to get full stakeholder representation of the process together for a project, and hence a more localized approach to change management is undertaken. Also, with little solid data available on which to base decisions and with just simple tools at hand, versus more advanced data-driven change methodology, decisions are often primarily based on gut feel. This is known euphemistically as "basing decisions on experience." Managers (incidentally who are measured on making change) pull teams together ostensibly to implement a known solution (usually theirs), and any examination of data is done purely to provide grounds to do so. With this localized and biased viewpoint, little is done to gauge the potential impact of the solution, and even less is done to proactively examine beyond this one solution, let alone to examine the broader solution space.

Changes made on conjecture without context of any kind in high-stress environments are likely doomed to failure when glitches inevitably come along—the changes are not based on any form of evidence and thus are prone to a reversal of subjective opinion and support when things don't go quite as planned. Any initial support quickly wanes, and the focus is on trying to find another solution.

Many symptoms described in this chapter play off each other. For example, as mentioned earlier, benchmarking without context is a common practice. New processes are brought in without an understanding of the old process's needs or the new one's capabilities. Similarly, again described earlier, focus tends to be on people and not the process, so any process context is lost when people are the primary focus. The same thing applies to the systems-versus-process discussion. If the focus is on the supporting system and not the process, the context

---

6. In Dr. Deming's words: "85% of problems in performance can be attributed to poor processes rather than people. The role of the manager, then, is to change the process, not badger the people."

of process understanding is not addressed, and changes are made without the foundation of understanding required.

ADDING VERSUS SUBTRACTING (PATCHING)

In most industries there are process engineers, a professional role whose primary focus is to design operations processes from scratch, considering the needs of customers, linkages to suppliers, process activities, controls, and so on. This role is rare, if not entirely missing, in healthcare. Healthcare processes tend to evolve over time, and if very little is ever done to take them apart and streamline them, they grow ever more complex and unnavigable, forever being tweaked and added to.

To ensure the right level of performance, quality groups often take on a kind of "process police" role, belatedly tracking the symptoms and reacting when the process goes awry. As more and more is added to the process, the related burden of work content increases accordingly, and the encumbered staff find it harder and harder to focus on (or even see) the critical elements amid the process noise. When the focus is on people, patching occurs differently from unit to unit and shift to shift. This inconsistency, coupled with the higher complexity of an overburdened process, leads to decreased process reliability; that is, the same processes are executed differently between units, shifts, and personnel. Lower reliability in turn incurs extra policing, patching, and complexity, and the cycle repeats.

Simpler processes are more reliable. There is really only one process I can do reliably 100% of the time, and that is nothing.

POOR IMPLEMENTATION

Once a solution is identified with the test-and-tweak thinking, implementation is left to unit managers, and rollouts are often no more than a single-shot communication of the concept. Subsequently, each unit manager is left to construct the detailed design. Such uncontained implementation leads to no standardization or consistency across units or shifts or even individuals on the same shift. The target process gets a watered-down implementation at best.

In such an environment, where reliance is on the personalities involved, it is very likely that physical changes, systems changes, education, and changes in orientation packages are not fully implemented, and little emphasis is placed on inclusion of customers, suppliers, and key process stakeholders.

With an informal approach to the rollout of any change, every unit's processes are essentially different. This is readily apparent when implementing new information technology (IT) systems. The IT group is required to automate an existing, often flawed process, which varies wildly from unit to unit, is unclear, or often doesn't exist at all.

Also, with the disparate change groups prevalent in the industry, each group typically doesn't command enough resources to perform a robust rollout of a change. This is exemplified by the usual approach to rolling out new roles, which often involves an informal one-on-one verbal communication, not a carefully planned rollout of skill augmentation with the appropriate education, tracking of competency, and building the appropriate learning into orientation and transfer procedures. Such an ad hoc approach to skills and role change almost always leads to a difference in understanding of the changes across all those involved and hence considerable variation in the performance of the process.

No Emphasis on Control

Probably the most common questions and discussions in healthcare performance improvement currently are those centered on sustaining the gains from changes implemented. It appears that the vast majority of organizations are failing in this goal and much focus is placed here, from the numerous presentations at conferences to whole conferences targeting the subject.

The primary reasons for this failure are embedded in the failings of the traditional change methods described to this point, plus the lack of emphasis in traditional change models placed on control of the new process.

With multiple disparate change groups making change in the business, it is inevitable that a good process gets further tweaked by a subsequent change team. Individuals in the process are positively encouraged to tweak their processes (sometimes known as "simple tests of change") without context or data to validate their actions, contributing to the 1-sigma churn described previously.

Even the commonly implemented PDCA change model itself is inherently designed to fail in controlling the process. The approach is one of cycles of PDCA with the clear intent to make change and then later return to the process to make further change. The process never settles, and the tendency (call it human nature if you will) is to assume that rigor in control isn't really necessary because "we'll be back around again here shortly."

The people-versus-process factor is also a key element in failing to sustain. By relying completely on the individuals involved in the process to maintain new performance levels, rather than changing the fundamental physics of the process, staff either burn out trying to maintain the new process given their unreduced workload, or their focus simply gets diverted elsewhere. With no link of process metrics to personal accountability, it is inevitable that a process slides back to its original state.

With the divide between the quality group and operations groups, the sheer stress of pulling the team through the process to the point of implementation takes its toll, and the team, not given the task of placing robust controls, get dragged on to the "next thing" before control is even considered.

With all of these inherent flaws in the change model, it is absolutely no surprise that change is not sustained; in fact, it would be remarkable if it were.

MANAGEMENT VERSUS LEADERSHIP

An interesting difference between healthcare and other industries is the common confusion between the roles of management and leadership.

In healthcare there is often a department manager and a department director (the would-be leader). Oftentimes both are engaged in performance improvement, sometimes in alignment, sometimes not. Some days the director gets closely involved in the day-to-day running of the department, others not.

In other industries these roles tend to be more clearly defined: management is about tactics and consistency; leadership is about strategy and change.

The key sustaining role in healthcare is missing: both the manager and the director are measured on process improvement, that is, change. If the manager is not focused on consistency, the push for standardization is lost, thus propagating the differences between care units, shifts, and even within a shift. The role of managers should be ensuring that the process is performed in a consistent manner, and thus their focus is on standardizing across the staff and ensuring that their skill base is grown to the necessary level.

Leaders, on the other hand, should not get too involved in the consistency of practice other than to hold the managers accountable for it. Leadership's role is to create the vision, to manage and resource the change in a contained way toward that vision, and finally to ensure that the appropriate framework of metrics is in place.

In the traditional healthcare model where roles are mixed, control of change is lost and the standardization of practice doesn't occur. Any performance improvement implemented thus fails to stick.

SUMMARY

What should be quite obvious throughout this chapter is that the failings of performance improvement in healthcare are no comment on the people, but rather on the methods of change currently in use. People in healthcare, like people in other industries, are smart, hardworking, and creative—but unlike in most other industries they are laboring under change management systems that are antiquated.

The failings of the existing change system are obvious when written in black and white as here, but for some inexplicable reason this is overlooked and the methods are just accepted as the best approach.

The fundamental problem is not the difficulty of making change in healthcare; it's the change model itself.

STRUCTURING CHANGE

Program Infrastructure

In the previous chapter we saw how many of the existing change paradigms contrive to undermine an organization's ability to improve performance. It's probably useful, therefore (to set some context), to describe what change practices we are actually seeking. In no particular order, change should be:

- **Transparent and "contained":** Change occurs in known, visible "chunks" or "packets," such as programs/initiatives (multiple related projects), projects, and events. For simplicity of writing, here we'll use the term *project* in the generic sense to represent any or all of these. These projects are clearly defined and scoped; they don't overlap, counteract, or clash with each other and are singly resourced in that no two groups are working on essentially the identical problem and could potentially or likely overwrite one another's efforts; and there is no fragmentation of effort.

  Change occurs within the projects down a predetermined path, such as a set of milestones or a specified roadmap, and so progress is obvious and visible (easy to track) and clearly understandable to all. These change projects also have a clear beginning and very specifically a clear ending. We'll discuss this in more detail in what follows (regarding the difference between continuous improvement and breakthrough change), but here, from a transparency perspective, we'll need to know when the planned change effort will be over, freeing up valuable resources to move on to other things.

- **Aligned:** Change projects are created and driven directly from the strategy and/or market needs, rather than commissioned independently of these things and aligned/linked afterward. The premise here is that the projects are born from the strategy (for instance) rather than being thought up separately and then connected back to the strategy after the event, to try to ensure that they are meaningful.

  We don't want the projects that are "most aligned" with strategy (of the projects we *happen* to have identified to this point); we want projects that are *the* strategic projects and are aligned because they came *from* the strategy.

  Project alignment allows us to gain resource alignment. Project alignment alone isn't sufficient (we'll need other considerations), but it is a necessary component.

- **Balanced and meaningful:** Change isn't limited in focus to a single business indicator; it targets all relevant business "pillars," bringing improvement to operations, quality, and finance where applicable. Quality isn't sacrificed for the sake of finance or vice versa.

  The goals that are set are challenging and worthwhile, targeting significant results and associated financial attribution where appropriate.

- **Made in light of the appropriate context:** Solutions are based on a clear understanding of the Voice of the Customer (VOC) and relevant data. There isn't a reliance on existing solutions-in-mind, and the teams have the latitude to create a composite solution on what effectively is a blank sheet of paper, rather than having to just benchmark and copy. They are free to explore the full "solution space" before selecting or constructing the final chosen solution.

- **Appropriately scoped and focused:** Change isn't locally focused, ignoring the broader context, but rather considers the end-to-end process, its flow, and overarching functionality.

- **Lasting and sustainable:** Project Teams identify and tackle root causes, with a strong emphasis on robust implementation and control. Implemented solutions are subsequently owned by the staff. Performance management methods align the measures placed on frontline staff with business scorecard goals, and the focus thereafter is on consistency and sustainability versus reinvention and change.

These elements are not likely to come together and occur by chance; they require active management and leadership by key individuals with the right skills, methods, and tools. Thus it's clear we'll also need the following:

- **Appropriate methods and tools within projects:** Efficient and effective tools are clearly sequenced to support the path of critical thinking from problem to solution. Tools are objective and data driven, ensuring that change is made in context as previously described, reducing the risk of missed opportunities or ineffective changes.

  Change is fundamental in nature as opposed to simply a patch or Band-Aid, and considerations are made for process, systems, and people (in both roles and competencies).

- **Appropriate methods and tools across projects (at a program level):** Projects are managed within a broader framework that helps leaders prioritize, adjust timing and resources, track, report, and respond to make needed course corrections. The tools used are effective and pragmatic and ensure that the portfolio of projects is well managed.

- **Professional leaders and change agents to lead and conduct change:** All personnel working within the framework understand their roles and are competent to undertake them, whether they are managing the portfolio, championing individual projects, leading a project, are members of a Project Team, or are a part of the workforce as recipients of changes.

  Project Leaders, as critical change agents, are considered as professionals, are full time, and are highly trained and qualified, working through team members and key stakeholders to realize improved business performance.

In a book on rebuilding capability, the key focus must be on successfully identifying, aligning, resourcing, and managing change. We mentioned previously some of the needed tactics of managing change, but let's also examine what we mean by change itself.

Change predominantly falls into two main categories:

- **Needed improvement on key business metrics.** For example, shortfalls in quality, financial, and service indicators require us to use targeted change activities to remedy those gaps in order to be successful in the marketplace. In simple terms, it is the change of making something better.

- **(Major) strategic infrastructure change required to build or rebuild our organization to take a new required form for future success.** Again, in simple terms, this means the type of change when we do different things. Instead of measuring progress using metrics, strategic progress is typically measured on achieving milestones. A common example might be the structuring and transformation from a traditional clinical practice to an Accountable Care Organization (ACO).[1]

We need to add to this the third, often overlooked, category of "no change":

- **Performance sustainability and consistency.** Not all change is good, as described in Chapter 1. This third category is the ability to maintain a stable performing status quo when the first two types of change aren't required.

Paradoxically, when we think of change, it's also critical to understand its counterpart: when it is appropriate and how *not* to change.

In this way we are considering three key facets of change, as shown in Figure 2.1, the balance among strategic change, performance improvement, and operational sustainability. An organization that manages this balance successfully has the ability to execute its strategy.[1] If it mismanages the balance, difficulties arise:

- Way too commonly there is too much focus on performance improvement of a plethora of metrics across the house, with the notion of having to be the best at everything. This is the single largest underlying cause of many of the problems described in Chapter 1; resources are sapped away across the organization and few remain and are available to bring about broad-stroke change. Also, the continual drive to improve results in a constant churn of change, completely undermining sustainability and in fact degrading the very performance we're trying to improve.

- If too much focus is placed on strategic change at the expense of the other two categories, it's likely we'll fail to get the basics right and lose valuable market share while we undergo our broad overarching change.

- Last, if our focus is too much on consistency, we'll have a good foundation for change, but we're failing to bring about the changes required to compete in the market or transform the organization.

---

1. Whether the chosen strategy itself is the right one to be successful long-term in the marketplace is an entirely different issue and not one we'll attempt to address here.

Figure 2.1 The three key facets of change

In their book *Blue Ocean Strategy*, Kim and Mauborgne[2] use the wonderful analogy of describing traditional businesses swimming in a red ocean (the bloody waters of competition) and the strategic desire to swim from those waters into the clearer, uncontested waters of a blue ocean and not having to compete. This is a profoundly different way of thinking about things. Rather than trying to win the game you're playing (against the odds), try to find a different game to play that no one or few are playing and hence dramatically improve your odds of success. Most healthcare organizations focus intently on life in the red ocean

---

2. W. Chan Kim and Renée Mauborgne, *Blue Ocean Strategy: How to Create Uncontested Market Space and Make the Competition Irrelevant* (Harvard Business Review Press, 2015).

and how best to compete while dreaming of yesteryear, when they didn't have to, and when they might again be in a bluer ocean.

Our three facets of change fit the red/blue ocean analogy well:

- Strategic change is equivalent to setting the blue ocean destination, mapping the course, and managing the change of the journey (tracking progress on our milestones).
- Performance improvement focuses on maintaining that necessary competitive edge to allow us to compete in the red ocean, to outpace the rest as we swim (tracking progress on key metrics).
- Last, our operational sustainability focus ensures our organizational health and well-being, our basic ability to perform every time—simply to be able to swim to survive.

Lean Sigma as described here, where organizations most often start out, fits perfectly in the category of performance improvement. As outlined in the Control Phase descriptions (later), it also brings or relies on key elements of process management as part of the sustainability of the newly implemented process.

Also over time, Lean Sigma Project Leaders become highly skilled project and program managers, grow quickly into the role of strategic project managers, and become an integral part of how the organization executes its strategy.

LEAN SIGMA: THE PROGRAM

To this point we've been purposely maintaining a generic (methodology-agnostic) perspective to ensure clarity of the underlying problems and the necessary components of the solution. Not surprisingly in a book with Lean Sigma in the title, the focus will be on the Lean Sigma approaches, but truly for the magnitude of the undertaking we have been discussing, there really isn't a lot of choice. It's worth making mention of another potential option often considered, namely, a Lean Transformation. This avenue is in practice a tougher one to take in healthcare, with less likelihood of success, despite at first glance seeming to be easier. Lean Transformation relies on mass change at a grassroots (frontline) level (versus the more strategic targeted change of Lean Sigma) and does work extremely well in many industries. It does, however, rely heavily on the ability of the in situ management system to sustain any change implemented. The management systems used extensively across most of healthcare are just not able to support such an endeavor. The leaders with the few strong successes in healthcare, such as at Virginia Mason Health System, even draw visitors' attention to their systems, but many overlook the true power of what is really in place and mistakenly focus instead on how the change events are led and by whom.

Thus, from here on the focus will be specific to one proven solution to the problems, namely, the deployment of a Lean Sigma program.

Now in the prior sentence, note the very specific wording: *deployment, Lean Sigma, program.*

- **Deployment:** This takes leadership to bring to an organization. In healthcare, Lean Sigma is often seen to be just a tool set or a very tactical, low-level activity, which immediately destines it to failure. Here we will consider the critical deployment elements to bring to bear on what is for most a very different way of thinking about change.

- **Lean Sigma:** The approaches described utilize multiple methods: Lean, Six Sigma, but also project management, change management, VOC, concept design and development, and process performance management among others. There is no place in the heat of battle for the purist view of a theorist. Methods and tools are selected and advanced based on their effectiveness and efficiency. This stuff works, but if something better comes along, it is a robust enough framework to embrace additional or replacement tools and techniques.

- **Program:** Lean Sigma isn't a set of tools, a roadmap, and a few projects. Instead, through a focused organizational infrastructure it is a business initiative or an underpinning to the way we do business or at least go about changing our business.

This isn't something that executive leaders delegate, because it's a cornerstone of leadership itself. It's the means to execute strategy; it's a means to meet market performance requirements and the means to manage sustainable performance.

It's not about the knowledge of some tools or data or analytics; it's a fundamentally different way of thinking, and as such for many organizations it becomes a compulsory leadership competency.

To reiterate, leaders should absolutely not delegate this. It is a key component of leadership itself.

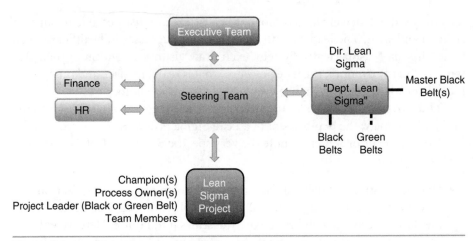

Figure 2.2 Lean Sigma program organization structure

At a program level a certain amount of infrastructure is critical for success. Many leaders new to Lean Sigma are misled into believing that all that is needed is a Project Leader trained in basic Lean Sigma tools and some projects to be successful.[3] Unfortunately, especially for those concerned, this is quite far from reality.

Figure 2.2 shows the basic organizational infrastructure required for a Lean Sigma program. The infrastructure can be thought of in two sections: the program level and the project level. Our focus in this chapter will primarily be at the program level, and our focus in the next chapter will be at the project level.

THE STEERING GROUP

At the core of the *program*-level infrastructure is the Steering Group, Team, Council, or Committee (all synonymous) that governs the program, sets its direction, selects projects and Project Leaders (known as Black Belts [BBs] and Green Belts [GBs]), and manages the overarching deployment, timelines, resourcing, and course correction. The Steering Group meets monthly after the first few months, but more frequently (biweekly or even weekly) as a program commences.

---

3. Most of the miscreant misleaders are from organizations that sell Lean Sigma training classes and for the most part have never seen a Lean Sigma program as such, or at least a successful one.

The Steering Team is typically made up of the following:

- **Executive Champion for the program:** One of the Executive Team, a C-level individual or vice president (VP), typically sits as the Chair of the Steering Group. The Executive Champion ensures that the Lean Sigma program is aligned with the business strategy and reports out on Lean Sigma matters to the Executive Team.

- **Other key executives:** The focus of the program may vary over time, and depending on this focus the relevant members of the Steering Group may evolve but almost certainly will include the executives (C-level or VP) over medical and clinical operations as well as finance and support function operations (diagnostics, pharmacy, materials, etc.).

- **Director of Lean Sigma:** In the early stages of a deployment, the Executive Champion likely takes this role, but once the program is stable and has enough impetus, it's a good idea to appoint a full-time person to the role. The Director takes on the more tactical aspects of the program and the day-to-day management of the personnel involved.

- **Finance representation:** Although the CFO may be a member of the Steering Group, it's important to have the involvement of a financial analyst in the program. This person is charged with ensuring that financial returns from the projects are identified, real, and tracked appropriately.

- **Human resource representation:** So many of the decisions of the Steering Group and the outcomes of the program and individual projects impact the roles of the workforce that having an HR role on the Steering Group is critical. As the program is deployed, emphasis is put on the newly created roles of Project Leaders. Considerations such as reward and recognition, career path planning, and personnel performance management are required, even before the staff members can transition into the roles.

- **Key change leaders:** Other improvement/change leaders, such as medical quality and clinical quality directors or the equivalent, ensure a common understanding of project prioritization and resourcing and ensure that change is conducted efficiently across the organization. The primary goal here is to reduce the clashing of disparate change groups described in Chapter 1.

Having such a steering body can seem like a tough addition to executives' already heavy workloads. As mentioned earlier, part of the justification here comes back to the simple realization that governing change is a key part of leadership and hence has to have time invested in it. Additionally, executives often query whether this should be an additional entity: "Why can't we just use an existing meeting to do this work?" The reasoning here is multifold:

1. The Steering Group isn't a meeting; it's an organizational body with organizational responsibilities. It is part of a flow of accountability that a simple meeting could not possibly achieve.

2. Most organizational leadership structures aren't agile or responsive enough to deal with the rapid changes and decision making required to launch and initially manage a Lean Sigma program.

3. Over time it is important to fold the Steering Group back into the existing leadership mechanisms. Most executives understand this, but to a one they realize, having managed change through a Steering Group, that the existing leadership mechanisms themselves are in need of updating and they gain a significant bolstering from the rigor and discipline learned from leading a program through the Steering Group.

Lean Sigma programs are thus most successful when initially launched as a free-standing infrastructure in parallel to the main organizational leadership structures. After typically two or three years or so, once the leadership and workforce understand what it means to have such capability in-house and the program has enough momentum and credibility, most leadership teams elect to consolidate the program infrastructure. This is done most often into the strategy planning and execution infrastructure.

In simple terms we light a small ember of a program on one side, nurture it to a good-size flame, and consolidate only when the risk of it being extinguished has passed.

SETTING THE PROGRAM DIRECTION

Most programs fail to make headway in the early stages primarily due to a lack of clear understanding of *why* we're doing this in the first place. A key first discussion of the Executive Team, even prior to the Steering Group being formed, is on the purpose and vision for the program, at a minimum answering these questions:

- What are we doing?
- Why are we doing it?

- What are the desired outcomes?
- What are the types of business problems that we expect to solve with this?
- How will this fit with other initiatives?

If the value of the program isn't discussed and agreed to up front, confusion will quickly arise, focus will be lost, and the program will begin down a slippery slope as other priorities appear on the executive's desk, as they certainly will. Once these questions have been answered, it's a good idea to use the responses as messaging in the initial communications to leaders, managers, and the workforce.

Every program purpose is likely different, but given that the primary value that Lean Sigma can immediately bring is improved performance, there is a useful common set of messages that could be incorporated here. In terms of the program purpose, we should be able to link directly back to the purpose of the organization. Consider the following:

In simple terms, any hospital or health system has two primary purposes:

1. To provide the best patient care today (short-term performance and consistency)
2. To provide the best patient care tomorrow (long-term growth and sustainability)

The term *best* is vague enough to include all aspects of the care experience such as quality, clinical outcomes, service, convenience, and so on, and the term *patient care* is vague enough to include all types of care from wellness to episodic and across the spectrum of acuity.

Most in healthcare readily understand the former, but the latter, even though understood at the executive level, is crucial and is often underemphasized in the context of the here-and-now further down in the organization, and in many cases it is rejected entirely. To satisfy this longer-term thinking, there needs to be an additional financial focus to support future care operations, along with a strategic consideration of long-term direction and identity of the organization. This matches well with the three facets of change described earlier (namely, strategic, performance improvement, and consistency/sustainability) and the notional strategic change journey toward a bluer ocean.

At the launch of most programs, the focus probably won't be the strategic infrastructure changes but more likely will be the competitive performance elements required to survive and ideally thrive in the market—that is, the ability to compete in the red ocean. This ability to compete is certainly not limited to quality performance, which is sometimes how leaders think of Lean Sigma—"just

Table 2.1   Major Metrics by Which a Lean Sigma Program Might Be Focused[4]

Metric	Description
Revenue	Monies generated from reimbursement for services rendered, from self-pay patients, private insurance, Medicare, and Medicaid.
	Relates to growth, e.g., compound annual growth rate (CAGR), market share, and effectiveness.
Profitability	Monies remaining from revenues after the costs of delivering the service (labor, materials, facilities, professional fees, etc.) are subtracted.
	Relates to margin, productivity, and efficiency, for example.
Working Capital	Assets in the form of cash reserves, long-term investments, equipment, facilities, etc.
	Relates to timeliness of billing and days in accounts receivable (A/R), for example.
Customer Satisfaction	Patient satisfaction and physician satisfaction as measured internally by operations groups or by external benchmarking organizations such as Press Ganey and Gallup.
Quality	Clinical quality measures such as mortality and morbidity, etc. Inclusion of this is debatable in that it drives the other metrics, but it is generally considered important enough to call out separately.[5]

another quality initiative; something to delegate to the quality folks while the leaders can get on with the important aspects of running the business."

Thus, Lean Sigma efforts should be driven and prioritized against a balanced set of business goals, including patient-centered, operational, and financial goals. These are generally framed around major metrics such as those shown in Table 2.1.

Only recently, with the advent of healthcare reform, has the notion of a truly balanced view including financial metrics become possible with healthcare leadership; however, as the majority of U.S. hospitals are not-for-profit, emphasizing the financial aspects of healthcare provision is still disturbing to many in the front lines. The famous adage "No margin, no mission" is apt here, but why is this so important? Without profit and the subsequent cash amassed,

---

4. Note the purposeful omission of measures of employee engagement or satisfaction. Again, this will be discussed in the metrics section of this chapter.

5. Relates to clinical outcomes, not process compliance metrics. This requires a further discussion and will be broached in the metrics section of this chapter.

a hospital cannot afford to invest in new technologies, facilities, staff, expansion, marketing, and other assets. A business that isn't growing is dying (costs will eventually catch up and place the organization in financial hardship), or the competition will slowly capture more of the market share, which amounts to the same thing.[6] Also, given the huge changes required to function in the transformed landscape, the vast majority of organizations are undergoing massive restructuring, consolidation, or rebuilding, which again requires significant investment on their part.

Thus the relevant metrics as shown in Table 2.1 are business metrics, not just clinical or quality metrics. Lean Sigma is a business initiative, not a quality initiative. So, being a little flippant, simply put, all a hospital or health system has to do is grow, while at the same time maintaining customer satisfaction and profitability, thus ensuring adequate cash reserves. Easy to say, obviously not so easy to do.

At this point, traditional performance improvement and Lean Sigma are already beginning to diverge. The traditional focus is typically on improving the clinical performance and quality, whereas Lean Sigma takes a more business-rounded view. Throughout the whole Lean Sigma approach, there is no distinction between quality and operations improvement. Quality improvement is achieved through operations improvement, because obviously the quality of care is created in operations. This brings a significant unification to all performance improvement in the organization, rather than having improvement being made by disparate, sometimes competing groups as described in Chapter 1.

THE FIT WITH EXISTING INITIATIVES

Another key consideration is the fit with other existing initiatives. This aspect is obviously highly dependent on exactly what those other initiatives are, but the most common question to answer is whether Lean Sigma is part of a broader performance excellence initiative, is one of many parallel initiatives, or is the umbrella program under which other initiatives fall, as depicted in Figure 2.3.

The answer here depends on many factors such as what the executive would like to achieve from the program, the strength of brand of the existing initiatives, and other factors. Some organizations go to great lengths to describe just how things fit together. One example of the no-umbrella approach is how a medium-size hospital initially positioned its Lean Sigma projects and program.

---

6. An example of this in a hospital radiology unit is described in Chapter 4.

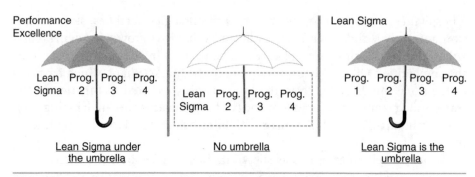

Figure 2.3 Lean Sigma's fit with other performance excellence initiatives

At the time (around 2005), the program was embryonic and there was little organizational understanding of what could be achieved through it. Like the majority of their counterparts at the time, the hospital leadership was very much focused on swimming in the red ocean, trying to compete to win. The multi-layer diagram in Figure 2.4, affectionately dubbed the "wedding cake" due to its look, shows how they linked multiple active programs (including Lean Sigma) back to strategy.

They had purposely chosen a strategic goal of "be the best at everything we do," a lofty goal, but it really helped to drive performance improvement in the organization. To make claim to being the best, there had to be measures involved; otherwise, how would they know they were the best? These were provided from various external sources such as Magnet[7] and *Fortune*, as well as internal benchmarks such as physician satisfaction, as shown in the second layer in the figure.

An interesting and correctly placed inclusion in the external benchmarking group was Baldrige.[8] Quite often healthcare professionals mistakenly think that Baldrige is an improvement methodology, with statements such as "Should we do Lean Sigma or Baldrige?" Baldrige does not in fact provide the means to improve but does, however, provide a means of judging current systems performance and an objective way of identifying opportunities for improvement that can be tackled using improvement methodologies such as Lean Sigma, or strengthening of an organization's management systems.

---

7. The Magnet Recognition Program, operated by the American Nurses Credentialing Center, recognizes healthcare organizations that provide excellence in nursing.

8. The Malcolm Baldrige National Quality Award recognizes U.S. organizations in the business, healthcare, education, and nonprofit sectors for performance excellence.

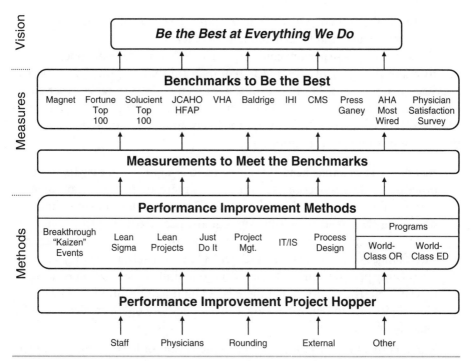

Figure 2.4 Example of how Lean Sigma is aligned to strategy[9]

The "Methods" row shows how the hospital leaders positioned the different kinds of performance improvement, including Lean Sigma, parallel to one another, which helped staff understand how these facets might work together.

Incidentally, since 2005 things have changed substantially once Lean Sigma found a footing in the organization. The hospital became a benchmark organization for Lean Sigma deployment and results. Most recently (2013 to the present) the Lean Sigma department has been transformed into the Office of Strategy Deployment (OSD), ensuring that all change is structured and aligned to strategy, resourced appropriately, and tracked and managed to success.

SHAPING PROJECTS

Before we can discuss where opportunities arise, it's important to understand what projects (as our means to take advantage of those opportunities) are and

---

9. Adapted from and used with kind permission from Columbus Regional Health.

how to think about them. Once we understand the shape of projects, only then can we develop them and launch and manage them.

The means to close performance gaps includes a rounded portfolio of methods to make change. Not all projects require a full-blown Lean Sigma project approach, so once project opportunities are identified, a suitably experienced group of individuals (typically a subset of the Steering Group augmented with a Master Black Belt [MBB][10]) decide on the likely approach required. There are a number of possible project options:

- **Just do it:** The change needed is known and is a quick and easy fix to the process. No data collection is required, and there are no significant organizational barriers to making the change. There is a clear, obvious, and unanimously agreed-upon solution that just needs to be implemented, and the implementation itself requires no significant project management. The change is effectively a "no-brainer." Unfortunately, many projects are mistakenly placed in this category. Everyone thinks the solution is straightforward, but the reality is that there isn't alignment in thinking. The best "just do its" are to remove or stop a current activity or effectively more of a "just *don't* do it."

- **Kaizen (also known as accelerated change event or breakthrough event):** The process needs to be streamlined to reduce complexity or improve flow. The problem doesn't require rocket science (or extensive data analysis); it just needs the right people in the room with a simple set of (Lean) tools and some good facilitation. These are typically three- to five-day events and are often aimed at capacity or throughput in areas with excess demand versus available capacity, such as computed tomography (CT) or cath lab.

- **Regular (engineering) project:** The solution is known and understood. The implementation takes time and resources, and thus a disciplined project management format is used to ensure success, for example, building a new emergency department (ED). Note that these projects often could be supported by Lean or Lean Sigma activity such as ensuring that the new ED design supports the right workflow.

- **Lean Sigma project:** The solution is not known and when discovered may take resources and time to implement. The problem is not one of simply reducing complexity; some data collection and analysis will be necessary. Lean Sigma projects will be explored in detail in Chapter 4.

---

10. More on roles later in this chapter.

- **Standardization project:** The process doesn't require major change; however, many of the staff conducting the process do it in different ways. The problem is thus one of setting a standard process and having all of the staff follow it. Standardization projects will be discussed in Chapter 4.

- **Process design:** The process itself isn't defined or may not exist at all, or the current process technology may not be capable of the performance levels needed. A whole new process is required.

- **Service development:** The organization would like to develop a service (or product line) to move into a new market. A project is undertaken to understand the strategic intent, understand the market, and target customer needs and shape a new service accordingly. Once developed, such projects often spawn multiple Lean Sigma projects or Kaizens to improve performance or increase capacity in adjacent processes to better support the new service.

- **IT/IS project:** The organization has identified a new or replacement information system need, and a project is undertaken to understand the process requirements (and thus the system requirements), develop the system or identify and tailor it, and then implement it. In more mature Lean Sigma organizations it is required that a Lean Sigma process improvement project be undertaken prior to any IT/IS work, to ensure that the Voice of the Customer (VOC) and Voice of the Business (VOB) are deeply understood, but also to determine if the new system is needed at all.

- **Programs:** In some cases such as in the ED or in surgery there are many related projects that should be dealt with as a set of projects rather than individually. Creating a "world-class OR" or "world-class ED" program as an umbrella initiative to provide oversight for multiple related projects ensures the correct integration of projects and a reduction in total resource effort.

FOCUS ON PROCESS

We saw in the previous chapter that the traditional improvement approach often involves multiple uncoordinated teams to tackle symptoms as if they were unrelated. Here the approach is very different.

Lean Sigma is a *process* improvement methodology, not a *practice, symptom, function,* or *activity* improvement methodology. This is a key distinction in framing projects, and it is one that newcomers frequently get wrong during project identification, scoping, and selection.

Practice relates to what needs to have been achieved during a time period and why. For example, if a patient arrives at the ED with chest pain or a heart attack, practice describes the "what" (patient receives a fibrinolytic drug within 30 minutes of arrival) and the "why" (to open the clogged artery and minimize heart damage). The process relates to how the practice is achieved, when, and by whom, in this case by the ED nurse during triage from the storage cabinet to the left.

A process is a sequence of activities with a definite beginning and end, including defined deliverables. Also, a "something" travels through the sequence (referred to as an "entity"), typical examples being an order, patient, or bill. Resources are used to accomplish the activities along the way. If there is no obvious, single process identified or if the process doesn't have a start, an end, deliverables, or an entity, it probably isn't a process and you would struggle to apply Lean Sigma to it.

Figure 2.5 shows an extended version of Figure 1.1's description of processes and systems to include the roles (analogous to the seats people can sit in through the process), the competencies required to sit in those seats, the people having those competencies who sit in the seats, and the knowledge base that supports this. Lean Sigma projects focus on the process aspects of this picture but by necessity have to work through the connection to systems, the roles involved, competencies, people (typically staff), and the supporting knowledge base.

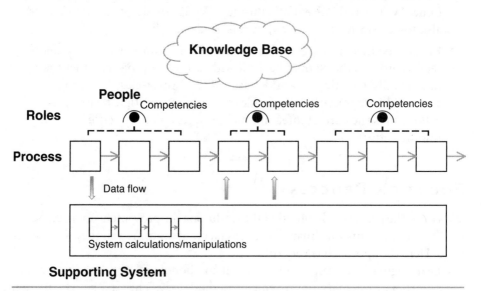

Figure 2.5 The relationship between processes, systems, roles, people, and competencies

BREAKTHROUGH CHANGE

One of the most common mistakes made with respect to change in healthcare relates to the notion of continuous improvement. As described in Chapter 1, continuous improvement has become synonymous with everyone being encouraged to make incremental change all of the time, in an effort to gain a continuously improving performance like that shown on the left in Figure 2.6 (see page 36). An initial endeavor to improve performance from a low level can yield improvements, but a logical disconnect arises when leaders and staff believe that continuing to change will bring yet better performance, when in reality it is much more likely to get worse.

This flawed thinking has given rise to continuous churn in organizations with processes not stabilized or controlled and has in fact led to reduced performance. Lean Sigma can be thought of as continuous improvement, but referring not to change at the process level (staff continuously tweaking the process), but rather at the organizational level as a whole. Breakthrough change is made process by process and as a result the organization continually improves.

Lean Sigma from a single-process perspective is a breakthrough change approach, as depicted on the right in Figure 2.6. A change Team is launched based on a business need. The Team works to understand baseline performance (no immediate change is made). The Team then determines the context of why the process performance is the way it is (and still no change is brought about). Next, the Team designs and develops the new process, along with a robust implementation plan. Only then is change made—not just a minor (hit and hope) tweak, but instead a significant change in the context of understanding what is really driving process performance: a breakthrough change. Once that change is made, focus is placed on locking down the process, so no subsequent change is allowed and the elevated performance is sustained.

The word *breakthrough* is obviously a little vague, so in an effort to clarify, Table 2.2 shows real examples of performance change made using Lean Sigma.

PROJECT TIERS

How projects are structured, the approach, the resourcing needed, and the quickness of return all depend on the complexity and magnitude of the process(es) being targeted. The complexity of projects can be categorized into three levels or tiers, with Tier 1 being the least complex and Tier 3 the most (see Figure 2.7 on page 38).

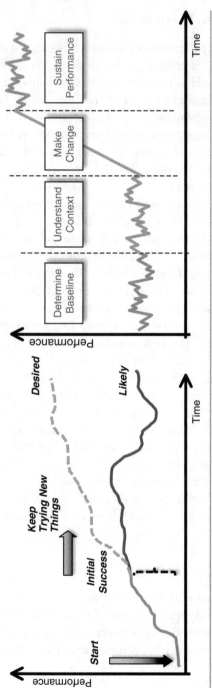

Figure 2.6 Continuous improvement (left) versus breakthrough change (right)

Table 2.2 Examples of Breakthrough Change in Healthcare Processes

Process	Metric	Result
Medication Delivery	Time from order written to nurse aware	60% reduction
	Accuracy (right med, right location)	99% defect rate reduction
	Phone calls between pharmacy and care unit	50% reduction
Emergency Department	Average length of stay	40% reduction
	Left without being seen	80% reduction
	Gross margin	20% increase
	Reimbursed revenue	$1.1 million increase
Radiology (CT)	Cycle time	40% reduction
	Capacity	Five-fold increase
	Reimbursed revenue	35% increase
Cath Lab Charge Capture	Reimbursed revenue	$3.8 million increase

TIER 1: PROJECTS

Tier 1 projects are those where the process is usually geographically well defined and relatively small in scope. The process can be tackled independently of other processes, with no domino or cascade effect whereby this process issue could not be resolved until other (adjacent) process issues are tackled. The project can be stand-alone. Tier 1 projects are often great training projects, good in the early stages of a Lean Sigma deployment.

The shape of the Tier 1 project may be different based on the type of process problem, whether it be flow related or perhaps an accuracy issue.

If the problem is flow related with a need to accelerate the process, Lean methods are likely the appropriate approach and a Kaizen event an appropriate vehicle.

As an example, a hospital may wish to improve the capacity of its diagnostic imaging department. A Kaizen event might address the velocity of patients through the process and deliver significant results in increased volume, revenue, and patient satisfaction.

Some projects target an improvement in accuracy (or the reliability/robustness of a process), which includes examples such as reduction in incidents of catheter-acquired urinary tract infection (CAUTI), or perhaps a reduction in billing errors in a particular department.

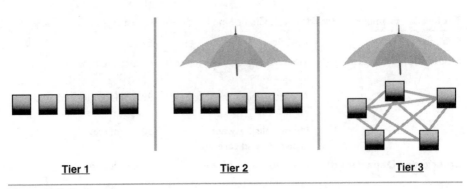

Figure 2.7 Project tiers

In this case, the problem is not simply one of streamlining or removing complexity. Lean Sigma, over a purely Lean approach, would be more appropriate, with its attention to reducing defects and minimizing variation alongside streamlining the process.

TIER 2: PROGRAMS

In contrast to Tier 1 projects, Tier 2 work is more aptly referred to as a program, in that multiple, smaller projects fall under a program umbrella. Tier 2 programs typically address a series of linked processes, often across several departments or functions, but in which there is a single primary flow.

The key characteristic of Tier 2 projects is that the bigger problem can be decomposed into subproblems and projects that are appropriate to tackle and be resolved independently of one another. In other words, they are a group of Tier 1 projects falling under a common umbrella.

A clinical example of a Tier 2 program might be a surgery process, from patient registration to discharge home or to a medical-surgical unit. This represents a relatively straightforward, sequential, linked process, at least from the patient's perspective. Other clinical examples might include the pharmacy process for medication delivery.

A nonclinical Tier 2 project might be the billing process. Successful completion of billing requires the coordination of many distinct processes across an overarching function. Charge capture is related to the billing process but could become its own Tier 2 project.

A useful approach to tackling Tier 2 projects is to begin with a Discovery event. Here, the overarching process is broken apart into its individual, discrete processes, performance metrics are captured, and projects are appropriately sequenced. Once the discrete subprojects are determined in the Discovery event, leadership collaborates to make decisions about sequencing and methodology for the ensuing program of projects. Some processes may be amenable to single Kaizen events, as in Tier 1. Other processes, however, may be more appropriately addressed by Lean Sigma projects.

Tier 2 programs also often include a VOC element. For example, for a Tier 2 surgery program, the team might interview surgeons and anesthesiologists to understand their experience with the existing processes, determine their key quality indicators, establish a baseline of their level of satisfaction with performance, and identify subsequent opportunities for improvement. These opportunities may form other projects under the program umbrella or serve to strengthen the process knowledge for existing program projects.

Tier 2 projects often call for their own Steering Committee made up of function leaders and process owners. The Steering Committee provides the guidance, support, and clout necessary for success.

A useful approach is to resource a Tier 2 program with a Black Belt as the program lead and multiple Green Belts to run the subprojects under the program umbrella.

TIER 3: COMPLEX PROGRAMS

Tier 3 describes large, complex programs within an organization made up of highly interrelated subproblems and processes that cannot be resolved independently of one another. There is a nominal umbrella, but the projects under the umbrella are so interwoven they have to be tackled as a single whole.

An example of a Tier 3 program is one that addresses patient placement and staffing. Such a program addresses multiple functions across the organization and cannot be fully decomposed into subproblems/projects that are resolved independently of one another, in this case:

- Patients categorized by need
- Room type and care requirement
- Patient placement process
- Staff assignment process
- Staffing models
- Patient demand by patient category type
- Skills matrix

Tier 3 programs require significant coordination and management across disciplines and usually follow an organizational redesign and transformation roadmap, not just a simple DMAIC[11] approach. They are not something to be tackled by novice change agents, and it is strongly recommended to use either an internal Master Black Belt or an external consultant equivalent.

IDENTIFYING OPPORTUNITIES

Now that we have a little more grounding in what projects represent and how to think about change, let's turn our attention to identifying opportunities. Our goal is to keep at all times an inventory of meaningful project opportunities in what is commonly referred to as the project hopper.

The sources of the projects aren't of utmost relevance, since all the projects will be prioritized against a common set of business criteria. The focus is on maintaining a meaningful set of potential projects at all times. It is worth noting that the hopper of potential projects is a source of great value to organizations. In fact, many CFOs, particularly outside healthcare, share the hopper contents and value with stock market analysts as a means of demonstrating their leadership direction and organizational potential and thus suitability as an organization for further investment (and subsequently to drive higher stock prices).

The organizational strategy should always provide a source of strong opportunities to populate the hopper. From the discussion earlier, note that there isn't a one-to-one relationship of opportunity to project; for example, a single opportunity might represent a Tier 2 program with multiple projects involved. So work is conducted to decompose or deconstruct opportunities into their constituent project parts before they are placed in the hopper and prioritized. This is quite a skilled endeavor, and it is recommended that an experienced hand be involved throughout. It's also useful to reiterate that opportunities should focus on process, represent a breakthrough change, and be as far as possible cast in a solution-free form going into the hopper.

Strategy isn't the only source of good projects. Shortfalls in performance in the metrics provide ample projects to fill any organization's hopper. Many of these performance shortfall opportunities are known already, but it is also useful to purposefully work to "mine" for these kinds of opportunities. This can be done in a number of ways, such as brainstorming in operational leadership

---

11. See Chapter 3 for a more detailed understanding of DMAIC.

team meetings, but a more rigorous route is through the development of an organization-level "Core Process Map."

The basic premise here is that any hospital or health system, despite having many hundreds of processes, is made up of a relatively small number of core, or mission-critical, processes, which form the fundamental building blocks or foundation. Consider them as the engine room of the organization. Each has an associated start, end, and known deliverables and performance metrics. These processes can be laid out in a high-level block diagram, our Core Process Map, an example of which is shown in Figure 2.8.

Creation of the Core Process Map requires considerable thought. These are not the typical functions of the business, which obviously aren't processes as such. An example here is the core process of medication delivery. Multiple functions are involved in this process from physician groups to pharmacy to nursing. The idea is to form actionable "chunks of process" to guide toward performance shortfalls.

For each process, measuring current performance (across the key process metrics) against benchmark or market requirements makes the gaps in performance apparent. These *processes* are now the opportunities—this is subtle, but very important; the focus is not on the metrics (which are symptoms) but on the processes that contain the causes for the metrics being at their current level. If the process does not change, the metric cannot change for any length of time.

Another source of projects that also links in nicely here is the organization's financial statements. The profit and loss (P&L) statement, or income statement, can help identify projects to grow revenue and reduce costs. The balance sheet can identify projects to free up cash. Examples of financially driven projects might include the following:

- **Revenue growth:** Increasing volume of patients, reducing "left without being seen" (LWBS), reducing cancellations, capturing lost charges, reducing contractual allowances
- **Cost reduction:** Reducing materials usage and obsolescence, reducing staffing costs (including overtime, on-call, and agency costs), reducing returned meal trays, reducing bad debt
- **Cash enhancement:** Decreasing A/R days, decreasing "discharged, not final billed" (DNFB) days, reducing materials inventory

By focusing directly on financials, the organization can create the means to deliver its strategy per Figure 2.1.

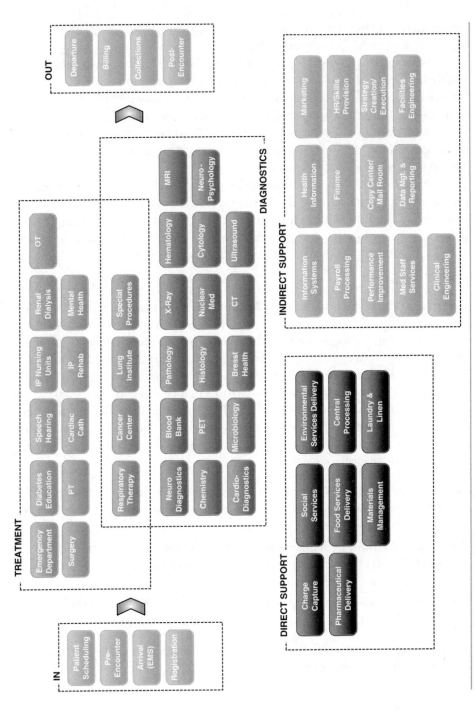

Figure 2.8 Core Process Map example

One final source of projects to fill the hopper is suggestions from hospital stakeholders (staff, physicians, etc.), rounding, and external sources such as consultants. These "bottom up" suggestions, as they are known, augment the "top down" projects developed from gaps in performance as related to the strategy. There is often an overreliance on this source. In reality, most frontline staff don't see enough of the end-to-end overarching context of business processes, and so these suggestions are likely too tactical or low-level. That isn't to say that all projects identified by this means aren't valid, but rather just be prepared to sift through a great many suggestions to find a few nuggets.

CHARACTERIZING PROJECTS (PRELIMINARY PROJECT CHARTERING)

Once projects have been identified, in theory the next obvious steps are to prioritize them and launch the most favorable ones. In practice, some work is required to clean up and characterize or clarify each project to enable the prioritization to be performed. Without this work, prioritization often is long and arduous.

Typically this step is conducted by the Program Director and one or more MBBs and involves putting a little more thought into the project focus. Some organizations prematurely hand projects to the Project Leader to put in this level of detail; however, this work should be done at a program level, well in advance of a Belt ever being assigned. In its simplest form, to characterize the project we'll need to know three things:

- A basic problem statement
- Project metrics and goals
- A likely Champion

This can be considered to be a preliminary Project Charter (a simple document to ensure that all the key players are on the same page regarding the project).

The problem statement should identify what particular problem this project is focused on solving. It will at least include what customers are being affected and what issue is affecting them, what is the impact on the customers, and when the problem occurs—in short, from a business perspective, why we should do this.

The approximate scope of the project is also considered, perhaps not in a precise way but more as a carving of larger endeavors into more manageable project pieces. This undertaking is known as decomposition or deconstruction.

The majority of projects are there to move a key business metric or metrics. Conventional approaches tend to use indicators such as

- Patient satisfaction
- Physician satisfaction
- Employee satisfaction

It is difficult to base improvement on metrics such as patient and physician satisfaction, because they are lagging indicators of the performance of the process. They are also impacted by a vast array of causes in the process and thus are very hard to isolate.

Employee satisfaction also warrants some discussion. Taken to the absurd, if I were trying to improve employee satisfaction, the perfect process environment for staff would be plenty of breaks, big-screen TVs, and Starbucks coffee for everyone. Clearly this is inappropriate. Conventional thinking leads us to believe that happy workers are productive workers. In fact, the reality is just the reverse from a cause-and-effect standpoint. The truer statement is "Productive workers are happy workers." Thus, a focus on the productivity of meaningful, value-added work is a key driver of employee satisfaction. If the process is streamlined and the work is clearly valued, workers are generally happier.

Another common metric approach is the use of percentiles relative to (similar) benchmarked organizations. They are useful for communication if we are doing well relative to others, but in practice they are poor guides. Even if we improve to the 99th percentile, so what? Is that good enough from a business perspective? Percentiles don't tell us in raw terms how much we need to improve or have the granularity we need from a metric. For example, when considering incidents of ventilator-associated pneumonia (VAP), zero incidents equate to the 99th percentile, and one incident might put you below the 50th percentile. Percentiles are also tough because they are moving targets—our raw performance can remain the same, but our percentile score can change as the performance of others in our benchmark group changes. For the most part they aren't specific enough and they're not actionable—it's important to get to the metrics behind the metrics.

Another ubiquitous approach is the use of compliance metrics, whereby the organization measures staff compliance or adherence to doing a particular process step or practice. These are typically used in lieu of process metrics. While this approach has worked well in many instances, such as VAP, it often overengineers the process (adds steps without improving performance).

Mostly the issue relates to the fact that even if there is compliance with an approach to 100%, so what? It's useful at this point to refer to a key foundation of Lean Sigma. Many process performance indicators measure outcomes of a process—let's call these our "big Y" measures. These Y measures are actually driven by many factors in the process—let's call these Xs. What we realize is that our Ys are just functions of the many Xs in the process, or in other words, they are just symptoms. All of these Xs probably impact the Y to some degree, but only a handful of Xs really make a big difference. The trick is to find the critical X or Xs and focus on those.[12]

Compliance often relates to a single X, which is just one of many and does not necessarily make a big impact on the performance measure Y; it isn't a critical X. A great example of this is the drive to comply with certain basic approaches such as AIDET[13] (Acknowledge, Introduce, Duration, Explanation, and Thank) to improve patient satisfaction. AIDET likely does have value in many cases, but the project is better framed in the light of the real reason for poor patient satisfaction, which could relate to many more overriding operational factors such as length of stay, number of stops in the process, capacity, accuracy, and so on. The tendency to keep revisiting the same X again and again to try to move the satisfaction measure will continue to be fruitless.

The obvious impertinent question here is why measuring whether someone actually did his or her job is a performance measure at all.

Thus, metrics used in developing and scoping Lean Sigma projects

- Relate to the performance of a single process (not an amalgamation of many processes)
- Are raw numbers, not percentiles
- Relate to the Ys for the process, not potential Xs (outcomes versus compliance)

Some examples include

- Lead time (e.g., the time it takes for a patient to progress the length of the process, such as a length of stay)
- Left without being seen

---

12. A wonderful example of this is described in the admission assessment case study in Chapter 4, where the simple X of whether the nurse hands off his/her phone to a colleague drives more than half of the process duration.

13. AIDET is a registered trademark of The Studer Group, LLC.

- Cycle time (e.g., the time between patients as they pass a certain point in the process, such as patient in to next patient in)
- Throughput (e.g., the number of patients processed per hour)
- Accuracy (e.g., percentage of orders processed correctly)
- Work content (e.g., hands-on time spent by a nurse per patient)

SETTING GOALS

Accompanying the metrics are the associated goals. Goal setting is a key difference in Lean Sigma, and if it is done right, it can dramatically impact program results.

Consider a common scenario, an emergency department with too long a length of stay (LOS). The current average is approximately 5 hours. The ED leadership have worked for some time to reduce the average and are now at the point of considering a Lean Sigma project to reduce the time further.

Traditional goal setting takes into consideration the struggle to this point and would seek to reduce the LOS by a reasonable amount, say, 30 minutes, the assumption being that if the team did manage a 30-minute reduction, perhaps they could work harder to squeeze a bit more reduction.

In reality it never seems to work this way. We try to make everyone aware of the problem and hope they'll work harder and make the difference. In reality we won't have fundamentally changed anything.

Let's take the analogy of a diet. I've been trying to lose 5 pounds for some time now. I do well for a week, or sometimes two, but then I always seem to slip back. Trying to lose 5 pounds is very tough. A few years ago my physician informed me of an elevated cholesterol problem. He advised me that I needed to change and change quickly. I looked at what I ate and just cut out all of the foods with high cholesterol content. I exercised a little more frequently, not much but something I could maintain. In short, I changed my lifestyle. I dropped my cholesterol from 285 to 135 (obviously a big relief), but also as a by-product I shed about 40 pounds in three months. It was actually much easier to do.

The same principle applies to Lean Sigma goal setting. Aim low and you'll probably not achieve it, achieve it and not value it, or struggle to maintain it. Aim for some loftier goal and there's a higher chance of achieving it and you're much more likely to maintain it. Another aspect of setting that high goal relates to staff and team engagement. The better goals are actually ones that induce responses like "That's not going to happen" or "You're nuts." If people don't know how to achieve a goal, they are much more likely to engage when we say we have the roadmap that will do it, and also they are less likely to independently attempt to achieve it themselves.

So how do we identify that lofty goal without being unrealistic? The approach taken is through the use of a concept known as entitlement. Entitlement is the best a process could ever be—perfection. For some metrics this is fairly straightforward:

- Yield: 100%
- Accuracy: 100%
- Scrap: 0%
- Defects: 0
- Errors: 0
- Cost of poor quality: $0

For other measures, it's a little trickier; for example, a round of golf has an entitlement of 18 (one shot per hole), not par as many people guess. For a process metric such as capacity, one approach might be that if we're running at 100% of capacity, the process is up all the time (zero downtime), going as fast as it has ever gone, and no time is spent doing rework.

Once we've identified the entitlement for the metric, we do *not* set that as the project goal. It would be wholly inappropriate to ask a Project Team to deliver perfection. Instead, the recommended approach is to set the goal at 50% of the way between the current performance and entitlement. For example, if current registration accuracy is 92%, the goal would be 96% (halfway between 92% and 100%). We often might also see a stretch goal of three-quarters of the way. In our registration example this would equate to 98% accuracy.

PRIORITIZING ACTION

As we know from any other project work, in pretty much every organization there just aren't enough change resources to form teams for all projects, and it is important not to stretch resources too thinly. It is much better to tackle a few projects and complete them quickly and efficiently than to tackle large numbers of projects in unison and have them drag out over months. Some prioritization is needed.

No.	Program	Project	Rating of Importance This Year							
			8	9	5	10	3	3	6	
			Profitability	Growth	Quality	Patient Satisfaction	Patient Safety	Staff Engagement	Regulatory/ Compliance	Total
1	OP Rehab	OP Rehab Capacity	3	9	0	3	1	3	0	147
2	Pharmacy	Antibiotic Stewardship	1	0	3	3	9	1	9	137
3	Clinical Documentation	2 Midnight LOS	1	1	1	3	1	3	9	118
4	Inpatient	Inappropriate Level of Care	9	0	1	1	3	1	3	117
5	CVOR	Charge Capture	3	9	0	1	0	0	0	115
6	Logistics	DME Billing, Charge Capture....	9	1	0	1	0	3	0	100
7	Pharmacy	Pharmacy Charge Capture: Duplicate Charges	1	0	0	3	0	0	9	92
8	SI/CUB	Post-Surgical Recovery Charge Capture	3	3	0	3	0	0	1	87
9	Clinical Documentation	Capturing CAUTI POA	3	1	3	1	1	0	3	79
10	Inpatient	Phase 2 of Med Rec	3	0	3	1	3	0	3	76
11	Emergency Department	ED DNFB—Process	3	3	0	1	0	1	1	70

Figure 2.9 Project prioritization matrix

Thus, once the opportunity processes have preliminary charters, they are placed in the project hopper and prioritized. This is done by rating the projects in the context of the major business metrics as shown in Figure 2.9, or even just on a simple urgency/benefit grid. Once the opportunities are prioritized, the top (more strategically important) projects focused on key process opportunities are obvious. Consideration of additional factors, such as cost, risk, and resource requirements, can help you fine-tune the selection. Projects are then chosen, teams are allocated, and projects commence.

PROGRAM AND PROJECT ROLES

At this point, let's assume we have selected a project and the approach will be to improve the target process, so we will need resources to launch the project to achieve this. Each Lean Sigma project has a

- Project Champion(s)
- Process Owner(s)
- Project Leader known as a Black Belt or Green Belt
- Team

The Project Champion is the sponsor for the project. The Champion should in essence be a customer[14] of the project and be senior enough in the organization to own the resources involved in the project and to remove barriers as the project progresses. Sometimes the Champion is the Process Owner (see below), but often not. There may be more than one Champion if the process crosses multiple functional boundaries. For example, for a medications delivery project, the Champions would perhaps be the director of nursing or preferably the chief nursing officer over the nursing units, along with the vice president over the pharmacy. If the project scope were to include physician activity, the chief medical officer would be a third Champion.

Clearly these are very senior people in a hospital, but this is the level of support needed (especially in the early stages of a Lean Sigma program) to drive results. If this level of individuals is not interested in the project, the project probably isn't strategically important to the organization and the organization would be better served by selecting a different project to tackle.

---

14. If the project is successful, the numbers by which the Champion is appraised will improve and therefore the Champion is aptly engaged.

The Project Champion meets early with the nominated Project Leader to define the project using a Project Charter. Project Leaders are known as Belts in Lean Sigma and typically fall into three categories:

- **Master Black Belts:** These are full-time resources who may undertake project work for perhaps half their time but are generally focused on mentoring other Belts through their projects, training new Belts, and leading awareness sessions for the hospital staff or helping manage the Lean Sigma program. Master Black Belts earn their stripes as Black Belts for at least two successful projects and then are trained with an additional three or more weeks of training in leadership, technical, and teaching skills.

- **Black Belts:** These are typically full-time resources whose primary focus is project work. Black Belts are trained for four weeks in the roadmap and tools described in Chapter 4. Black Belts can lead projects autonomously, and they quickly become skilled change agents. The projects undertaken can involve processes crossing multiple departments and be very complex in nature, both technically and organizationally.

- **Green Belts:** These are part-time Project Leaders. Due to the part-time nature of the role, the ongoing project learning cycles they have are less and so it's trickier for them to follow up on complex business issues and also to maintain a deeper skill base on the more complex Lean Sigma tools. For these reasons, they are restricted to fixing smaller pieces of a target process, or they are focused on smaller, simpler processes, perhaps within a single hospital function rather than across multiple functions. They thus have a lesser tool set (which still allows them to streamline processes and identify root causes of issues and resolve them). Training lasts for two weeks.

Both Master Black Belts and Black Belts (given that they have a full-time role) would report to a Program Director (typically a member of the Executive Team). In the early stages this role is played by a vice president or chief operating officer or similar.

Some organizations opt for a number of other Belt colors to represent other levels of experience such as awareness or the participation of an individual on a Lean Sigma team. Here we'll stick to the three main categories.

The Process Owners for the target process are the functional leaders for the areas that are crossed by the process. For the medications delivery process mentioned earlier, the Process Owners might be a care unit nursing supervisor and the pharmacy director.

The Team, as determined by the Project Champion, Process Owner, and Belt, is composed of key representatives from the functions involved in the process. The most apt Team members are those folks who "live and breathe" the process every day. They should be respected by their peers, since once the solution is constructed, there should be confidence among those not participating that their needs have been represented. The Team should be somewhere between three and seven members plus the Belt. Any more than this will make the Team unwieldy. Having a large Team isn't really a showstopper, but if necessary the Team can be whittled down by using multifunction resources—perhaps people who have experience in more than one discipline. The Team may also be augmented by ad hoc members, brought in to participate in certain tool applications or to validate process understanding. Teams contain all the right resources (at least in an ad hoc form), including operations, compliance, and clinical quality if appropriate. Note that the Project Champion and Process Owners are for the most part not included in the Team to ensure that Team innovation and objectivity aren't stifled by any sense of having to "say the right thing in front of the boss."

Lean Sigma differs from many typical project approaches in that the work is done *in* the Team meetings rather than *between* meetings, and any full Team interaction is focused mainly on progress reporting and planning the next actions. Hence, once the Team is formed, members meet for at least half a day, or preferably a whole day, per week, led and facilitated by the Belt. This is clearly a significant commitment and is often seen as a formidable request in novice Lean Sigma organizations. Remember, though, that the projects that might normally be under way in a fragmented form have been consolidated into a few well-managed, contained undertakings. Whole-day sessions generally make it easier to plan and backfill for staff involved.

There is sometimes a tendency to "shortchange" Teams by placing only available resources versus the right resources, or just allowing a Team member to participate when or if available. Having the right Team members is absolutely critical. Team members also need to be consistent for the duration of the project and not swapped in and out. The project work is a sequence of learning, so having a continuity of players is critical. Team members need to be freed up completely by backfilling or offloading their other activities or commitments. If the project is strategically important, it needs to be resourced accordingly. If resources aren't available, the Executive Group needs to take an interest in what other activities are under way and determine if any projects can be furloughed or consolidated.

In addition to the project roles, there are some key program-level roles. These include the Steering Group roles mentioned earlier (executives, program leader or director, financial analyst, HR, etc.) but also communication and education coordination.

For each role described, a key aspect of Lean Sigma is the competency required to conduct the role. Consider each role as a seat to sit in. Anyone sitting in the seat has identified accountabilities (goals and activities) and the associated competencies (and level thereof) to achieve those goals. Competency isn't considered just from the perspective of having it or not, but also by the degree or level of skill. Many in the organization may just need an awareness of or be oriented in a skill; some will need a higher level of skill to participate; some will need to be skilled in order to lead; some need to be skilled enough to teach; and at the highest level a few might be skilled enough to change the method itself.

Training, some of it quite substantial, is thus a key part of any Lean Sigma deployment to ensure that new competencies are ingrained. Chapter 5 deals more with the details of how this is planned and undertaken.

PROGRAM TRACKING, REPORTING, AND ONGOING MANAGEMENT

Managing the program on an ongoing basis involves managing across the portfolio of individual projects, and hence tracking and communicating (reporting) project status and results are an integral part of any Lean Sigma program. Lean Sigma projects follow a phased and gated roadmap, so it's possible to know the status of any and all projects at any time. Champions and Belts are required to report this status, typically on a monthly basis, to the Steering Group. Champions and the Steering Group manage the resource across the portfolio accordingly to remove roadblocks and ensure that projects progress in a timely fashion.

Financial tracking of implemented projects ensures that results are realized but also sustained in the months after each project closes.

Ongoing communication of project and program status and results to key stakeholders (leaders, staff, the Board of Trustees, etc.) ensures that the program continues to receive the attention it needs and to bear fruit. Such communication includes simple monthly statements and newsletters, CEO briefings, leadership updates, operational huddles, and annual reports.

SUMMARY

In simple terms, Lean Sigma as a program installs the key infrastructure elements that ensure that change is conducted and managed, meeting the criteria described in the first pages of this chapter—namely, that change is

- Transparent and contained
- Aligned with the business purpose and direction
- Balanced and meaningful

At the program level these elements ensure that projects are managed within a broader framework that helps leaders prioritize, adjust timing and resources, track, report, and respond to make needed course corrections.

At the project level, we'll see in Chapter 3 how Lean Sigma ensures that change is

- Made in light of appropriate context
- Appropriately scoped and focused
- Lasting and sustainable

LEAN SIGMA ROADMAP

The Anatomy of a Project

Chapter 2 described how to structure and manage change across projects at a program level. This chapter focuses on managing change *within* a project, specifically a Lean Sigma change project. At the end of the chapter, also briefly described are two other commonly used types of Lean Sigma project approaches, namely, standardization projects and accelerated change or Kaizen events.

First we turn to a Lean Sigma project, describing the way it is structured along with the thinking and approaches it relies upon.

LEAN SIGMA PROJECT ROADMAP

There are a multitude of incarnations of Lean Sigma, but for the purposes here it is best to consider it as the tight integration of two methodologies: Six Sigma and Lean. Both are business improvement methodologies, more specifically business *process* improvement methodologies.[1] Their end goals are similar—better process performance—but they focus on different aspects of a process:

- Six Sigma is a systematic methodology to home in on the key factors (known as Xs) that drive variation in the performance of a process (the

1. This may run contrary to popular belief that Lean Sigma is a quality initiative.

measures of this are known as Ys), set them at the best levels, and hold them there, thus ensuring a significantly increased performance level for all time. Six Sigma is an excellent method to drive much higher reliability in a process by increasing accuracy and decreasing defects.

- Lean is more of a collection of methodologies to reduce the complexity in a process and streamline it by identifying and eliminating sources of waste in the process, waste that causes a lack of flow. Lean is an excellent approach to increase capacity and throughput of processes, to help processes "move" better.

Another helpful way of viewing the difference is that Lean looks at what we shouldn't be doing and aims to remove it; Six Sigma looks at what we should be doing and aims to get it right the first time and every time, for all time.

The most common misconception at this point is that Lean, Six Sigma, and the integration of the two are simply toolkits. This is just not true. Admittedly there are tools involved, but viewing them as just toolkits is similar to defining a sports car as a collection of pieces of metal, plastic, and rubber. The identical materials might be put together completely differently and form something entirely different. The value is in how they are put together, but also in the "essence" of the sports car. The car is much more than the sum of its component parts.

In this vein, Lean Sigma is actually a way of thinking. It's a sequence of thought through a project that allows a team to progress from problem to implemented solution. Tools are used at every step along the way to answer the questions at hand, but it's the sequence of questioning (the flow of critical thinking) that is the backbone of the method. It is by this means that change is managed throughout the project.

This is a profound concept that many never even recognize, but for a leader planning to bring Lean Sigma successfully to an organization, understanding it is key.

On many occasions I've heard leaders say that they want to train everyone in the organization in the tools, so "they can pick them up and use them in their daily work." Ideally at this point in the book, you'll have realized that this statement really isn't advisable. Lean Sigma is a way of thinking and managing change. Just giving the raw tools to staff members would be at least inefficient, but more likely even detrimental to the organization. Uncontained, unfocused change made without the backbone of critical thinking and big-picture context can only lead to reduced performance and frustration of staff.

As we left off in Chapter 2, the project had been identified and the preliminary Project Charter drafted. The project Champion was identified, along with a Project Leader or Belt to facilitate the project. Next, a team of process experts is identified, staff who live and breathe the process every day. The Team follows a disciplined roadmap of five phases: Define, Measure, Analyze, Improve, and Control, often known by the acronym DMAIC. The roadmap is supported at every step by the use of multiple data-driven tools to systematically understand the true problem at hand, determine the reasons for the exhibited performance shortfalls, develop an appropriate solution, and implement it.

Briefly, for each phase:

- **Define:** Is this the right project? Is this the right project now?
- **Measure:** How is the process performed? How well is the process performed?
- **Analyze:** Why is the process performing this way?
- **Improve:** What should the new process be to perform the right way? The newly performing process is in place.
- **Control:** The performance is at the level it needs to be. The performance is stable and guaranteed.

The roadmap is structured into three layers:

- Major phases
- Subphases or steps (the goals or the "what")
- Tools (the "how" to achieve the "what")

A high-level representation of the Lean Sigma roadmap containing just the major phases and steps is shown in Figure 3.1.

Each of the major phases is divided into two to four steps. Each of these steps is not described by the tools that constitute it, but rather by the intended goals that the tools help achieve. Lean Sigma is really about linkage of tools to achieve goals, not using tools individually. The strength of the approach is in the sequencing of tools and the critical thinking based on goals.

The best level at which a leader should think of and interact with a Lean Sigma project is at the major phase and step level, as shown in Figure 3.1, rather than getting drawn down into the tools themselves too much. This leader interaction typically takes the form of "Which phase are you in?" and "What's between you and the end of the phase?" The discussion should be centered around the primary goals.

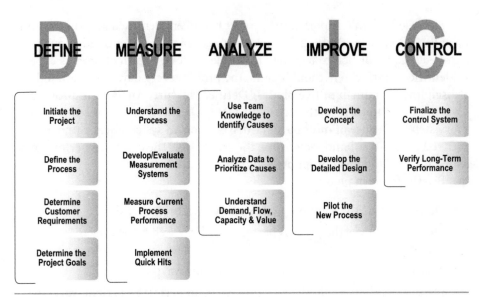

Figure 3.1 High-level Lean Sigma roadmap[2]

With this layered structure in place, the roadmap is goal driven, depicts the critical thinking sequence involved, and is completely generic as it relates to process performance improvement. The tools vary project by project, but these goals are consistent for all process improvement projects. The Lean and Six Sigma tools (and any others interchangeably for that matter) can be selected to meet the goals of any step.

The full roadmap with all three levels is shown in Figure 3.2.

As proven across a diverse range of companies, the roadmap is equally at home in service, manufacturing industries of all types, and healthcare, including sharp-end hospital and clinic processes, even though at first glance some tools may lean toward only one of these. For example, despite being considered most at home in manufacturing, the best pull systems I've seen were to control replenishment in office supplies. Similarly, workstation design applies equally to a triage nurse and an assembly worker.

The Belt progresses through the 16 steps in the overarching DMAIC roadmap, at each step utilizing the appropriate tools to meet the step goals. In this manner, the critical thinking involved in being a truly successful Belt is baked into the roadmap and guides each step along the way.

---

2. Source: © Haelan Group 2012.

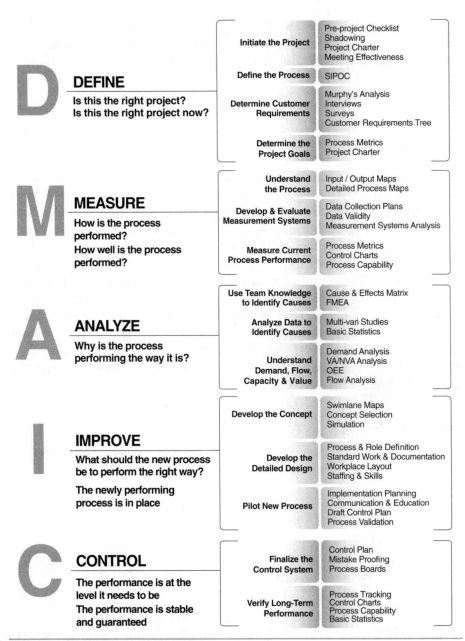

Figure 3.2 Detailed Lean Sigma roadmap[3]

---

3. Source: © Haelan Group 2012.

A good Belt always maintains the focus on the underlying principle of "I'll apply the minimum practical sequence of tools to understand enough about my process to robustly make dramatic improvement for once and for all in my process."

In the following sections we walk through each phase in more detail.

DEFINE

During Define, the primary objectives are to understand whether this is the right project and the best project to do right now. If not, it is either reshaped appropriately, postponed until it becomes a higher priority, or canceled completely. The Team is mobilized and spends time reviewing and making necessary updates to the preliminary Project Charter to ensure that everyone is on the same page as to what this project will address, its scope, benefits, who will be involved or affected, and what business value it will generate. Tools are used that begin to explore the process, its customers, their requirements, and the associated primary performance metrics. By the end of Define, the Champion, Process Owner, Belt, and Team are all on the same page with respect to the scope of the project, exactly what it will achieve (the problem it will resolve), and the business metrics by which success will be determined. The steps and supporting tools for Define are shown in Figure 3.3.

INITIATE THE PROJECT

Prior to the project commencing, the Belt, Champion, and Process Owner meet to formally hand over the project to the Belt to lead.

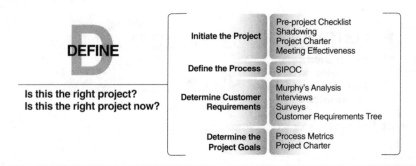

Figure 3.3 Define Phase roadmap

Lean Sigma is not a gladiator sport. The Belt is not there to deliver the project on his or her own. The Belt is a facilitator of the Team. *Initiate the Project* is when the Team first meets and the project is truly up and running.

The Belt is purposely selected to not be from the process area in question, primarily so that he or she has no preconceived ideas. However, the Belt does need enough of a basic understanding of the process layout, flow, and local process jargon to be an effective project facilitator. With this in mind, the Belt "shadows" in the area prior to the first Team meeting.

At the commencement of the first Team meeting, the Champion and Process Owners kick things off by introducing the Team to how Lean Sigma fits into the organizational strategy (or reminding them). They then explain to the Team the purpose, value, and initial scope of this particular project by walking the Team through the Project Charter. Once this is complete, the Champion and Process Owner are not part of the Project Team but check in regularly (at the end of Team meetings, for example) for "calibration."

DEFINE THE PROCESS

Although the prioritization process described earlier drove selection of a particular project, without more detailed insight into the process and its business impact the Team may not focus on the important elements. It is therefore important to have a well-defined scope for the project and that the true purpose of the process be understood. To define the process, the Team uses very simple mapping tools to determine the beginning and endpoints of the process to investigate them in detail and ensure the right scope.

DETERMINE THE CUSTOMER REQUIREMENTS

To determine the deliverables for the process, the Team could just accept the conventional thinking of what the process generates. Experience shows, however, that the purpose of most processes is misunderstood, and in fact large pieces of processes often exist to deliver things that aren't truly needed by the customers of the process. Often the true customers aren't identified or consulted on what is needed from the process. So, during the Define Phase, the Team uses a series of tools to identify the customer, gather the Voice of the Customer (VOC), and distill it into a usable form.

For the majority of projects this involves a series of carefully planned interviews to capture insight into the customers' worlds and their interaction with the process. The output is in the form of a Customer Requirements Tree, as shown in Figure 3.4.

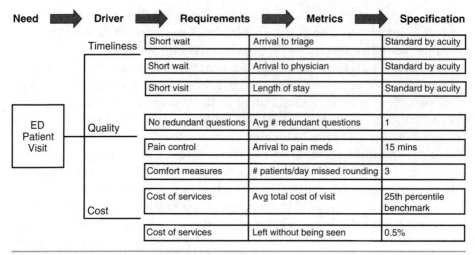

Figure 3.4 Example Customer Requirements Tree

It is worth mentioning that up until this step, projects for the most part follow the same path or tools sequence. This step, however, exhibits the first real divergence of tools by project. For example, if a project really has only a single, internal customer, the approach for capturing the VOC might be as simple as inviting the customer to a Team meeting and having an open-ended conversation about the needs and purpose of the process. If, however, there are multiple customers (or external customers), it is highly recommended that the Team spend much more time, effort, and tools focused on whom to ask what and how.

A common mistake made during this step is to consider staff as customers. Staff will be taken into consideration later in the roadmap, but positioning them as customers at this point can skew the real purpose of the process and even prevent unneeded steps from being designed out.

Another key mistake is confusing what is wanted with what is needed—improving a process based on what customers say they *want*, which often is very much solution oriented and thus very diverse, as opposed to the fundamental underlying *needs* across customers, which are typically a lot more consistent. Henry Ford said that if he had only listened to what people *said* they wanted, he would have made faster horses. He understood that the real need was for better transportation.

DETERMINE THE PROJECT GOALS

From the VOC, the subset of major metrics that the project will target is determined and a baseline is taken, typically from historical data. This baseline is rudimentary at this time (later in the Measure Phase a more robust baseline is taken)—effectively at this stage it's just a rough-cut baseline to determine if there really is potential in the process (remembering the Define goal "Is this the right project?").

The metrics are very much business based and are typically split between effectiveness metrics (those that are customer related, such as quality or service level to customers) and efficiency metrics (those that are business related, such as cost per unit of service).

With the project metrics identified, it's a matter of determining the target or goal value for each metric. To accomplish this, the approach taken is that used in initially chartering the project as described in Chapter 2, using the concept of entitlement (perfection for that particular metric). The target is thus set at (for example) halfway between current performance and entitlement.

As a critical juncture in the project, any mistake here can cause serious ramifications later for the Project Team. The most common mistakes in scoping projects are the following:

1. **Boiling the ocean (too large a scope):** The circumvention for this is tricky to explain in an introductory text such as this, given the multitude of complicating factors. In simple terms, if you find yourself in a position of chartering a project across multiple processes (a Tier 2 or Tier 3 program), the project is too large and needs to be broken into pieces.

2. **Having too many metrics:** This is somewhat akin to "boiling the ocean." If attempts are made to tackle too many metrics in the process, the project may effectively be trying to address the whole golden triangle (cost, quality, and timeliness) all in one go. The same is true if the project targets changes in practice, process, *and* systems all at the same time. Both of these are possible but require an experienced hand and a carefully designed approach.

3. **Micro-focused projects:** A very common mistake, especially in the early stages of a Lean Sigma deployment, is for leaders to scope a project too small, often with the thought that doing so will help a Team get through the project more quickly and with a higher chance of success. The opposite can in fact happen. Because the project is very small, the business value is low and thus the Project Team meetings often get postponed due to other (now higher) priorities.

4. **Having a solution in mind:** This is likely the highest-risk mistake that is made. Typically a senior leader has a pet solution in mind, and the

assumption (similar to the micro-focused project) is that the Team will be accelerated if the focus is just to install the solution.

The business problem has root cause(s) driving most of the variation in performance. An all-too-common scenario is that the chosen solution does not address the critical root cause(s) and now there is a difficult situation. The Project Team is unnecessarily limited to examining those Xs circumscribed by the solution. The leader often blames the Team for poor execution, when the reality is probably that they did the best they could under the circumstances but the chosen solution just didn't impact critical Xs. If the solution did happen to make a big difference, the Team sometimes gets reduced credit because it was not their answer.

Either way, as a Team or a Belt, if you're being handed a solution to implement, you might have a struggle ahead of you.

Once the right metrics and target values are determined, the Charter is updated and the project passes through a formal gate meeting, with the Belt, Champion, and Process Owner present, to review and sign off on the Define Phase. Define Phase signoff indicates that all parties are comfortable with moving forward and this project is worth applying valued resources. There is a clear opportunity and the Team can continue on to the Measure Phase.

MEASURE

During the Measure Phase the Team works to understand the current state of the process through the use of mapping tools. Focus is placed on ensuring the reliability of the primary performance metrics and then a more robust baseline is established. Once a baseline is determined, if any quick hits have been identified, the Team can go ahead and implement them. The steps and supporting tools for Measure are shown in Figure 3.5.

UNDERSTAND THE PROCESS

Here the focus is to use simple and yet surprisingly elucidating mapping tools to understand the basic structure of the process and begin to understand its shortcomings. The mapping tools used vary depending on the problem at hand. If the project is about increasing accuracy or reducing defects, the maps help identify

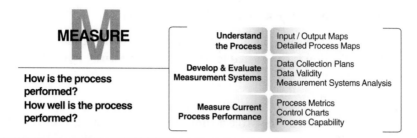

Figure 3.5 Measure Phase roadmap

all the potential Xs in the process. If the problem is more about streamlining and reducing complexity, the maps are more about detailing all of the individual process steps and delays.

Once the mapping is complete, the Team has a much deeper understanding of the current process, remembering that one of the questions to be answered in Measure is "How is the process performed?"

DEVELOP AND EVALUATE MEASUREMENT SYSTEMS

Measurement at this stage is aimed at the primary performance metrics for the process—just how good we are right now, before any changes are made to things such as cycle times and lead times. The prior mapping activities help determine exactly what to measure and where in the process, but before any data can be collected, work is undertaken to ensure that the metrics used are reliable. This means that they are clearly defined, repeatable (if I measure it more than once, I agree with myself), and reproducible (if two or more of us measure it, we agree with one another). This simple concept is remarkably powerful in identifying problems with how we measure performance of processes. It's very common to see lengths of stay not spanning the entire process from when patients walk in the door to when they truly leave the facility. Often we focus on a subset of the full process and hence limit our thinking and subsequently our results, or the data isn't captured or transcribed correctly. In most hospitals and health systems there is an abundance of data but very little reliable information. Disturbingly, when a request for data is made, it's common to hear the answer "Sure, what do you want it to tell you?" In the objective world of Lean Sigma, where data drives decisions, this obviously isn't ideal.

MEASURE CURRENT PROCESS PERFORMANCE

Once the measurement systems are proven to be valid and reliable, a carefully planned data collection is conducted for the primary metrics in the Charter. The purpose of taking the baseline is multifold:

- The process might actually be better performing than anticipated, and perhaps it's better to focus the project somewhere else—perhaps rescope the project or kill it entirely. Remember, "Is this the right project?" We need to make the best use of our valuable resources.

- The business cannot claim success for improving a process if it's not clear how good or bad the process was to begin with.

- More importantly (and this is certainly not traditional thinking), if a baseline is taken and improvement is made, the change in performance is truly understood. Once the project is complete, operators within the process are much less likely to try to "dink" with a process to improve it further if they understand just what a significant improvement has been made.[4] This represents one of the best control tools in Lean Sigma—processes tend to stay fixed because stakeholders in the process genuinely understand that the performance is better than anyone could achieve by additional tweaking. More importantly, this breaks the cyclical thinking attached to process improvement. Changes are made once and for all, and no one will mess with the process beyond this point unless some *external* factor or change drives us to do so.

During the Define and Measure phases often a lot of "low-hanging fruit" in the process becomes apparent. There is always a temptation to address these early in the project, but until a solid baseline is known, it's better to leave them for the three bulleted reasons just given.

Once a baseline measure has been taken, the Belt meets with representation from finance to formalize how the project will be measured financially. At a program level work will have been done in general to determine how key business measures (e.g., increased volume, reduced inventory, etc.) should be translated into dollars. At this point in the roadmap the financial translation is formalized for this specific project.

Financial analysts are also extremely helpful in identifying other potential value in the project.

After the financial review, the Belt, Champion, and Process Owner(s) meet to sign off on the final scope, baseline, and goal of the project.

---

4. Remember that most "dinking" leads to a degradation in performance.

IMPLEMENT QUICK HITS

Once a baseline has been determined, some quick hits can be implemented and quite often dramatic improvements can be made in a structured way.

Interpretation of what constitutes a quick hit varies considerably. Here it is defined as something that requires no analytics, has full consensus, requires few to no resources to implement, and can be rolled out very quickly.

By this definition, quick hits include only changes that are blindingly obvious. If there is any debate about the validity of a quick hit, it is no longer deemed as such. If a large number of resources are involved in the process, for example, in nursing, there is really no such thing as a quick hit. By the time the education plan has been developed for the quick hit and all the resources have been trained, many weeks may have passed and the project has likely progressed well into the Improve Phase.

A great example of a quick hit that I often share with new Project Leaders was in a returns process in an electronics business in San Diego, California. Customer service representatives (CSRs) would answer the phone and take details from customers regarding the return. They would fill in the paperwork and dutifully take a copy to the warehouse because "the warehouse needed it." The warehouse staff would likewise dutifully file the copy because "the CSR needed it filed." In reality all of this paperwork filling out, transporting, and filing was a total waste of time and money, and the simple quick hit was to just stop doing it. No analytics or investment was required, and it was a simple implementation.

ANALYZE

Analyze is designed to provide the context for the improvements to be designed in the Improve Phase, not as is sometimes believed to prove that an initial solution idea was correct. The Team uses data-driven tools (some statistical, some flow related) to understand the key sources of variation and waste in the process.

Analyze is the only phase where there is some separation of the methods of Lean and Six Sigma.

For projects specifically targeting the accuracy and robustness of a process, Analyze utilizes a sequence of tools involving initially Team insight and subsequently data collection and analysis to systematically home in on the critical Xs driving that accuracy. Later in Improve, focused change on these key Xs will significantly reduce defects in the process, thus making it more robust. The whole approach for accuracy and reliability projects is thus like a funnel, as shown in Figure 3.6.

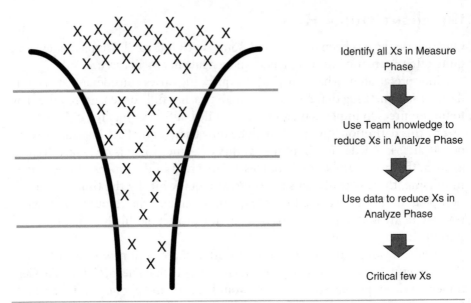

Figure 3.6 Funnel approach to identifying critical Xs

For flow/capacity-related projects, Analyze tools aim to identify the key sources of waste (hindrance to flow and reduction in capacity).

The steps and supporting tools for Analyze are shown in Figure 3.7.

USE TEAM KNOWLEDGE TO IDENTIFY CAUSES

For projects targeting accuracy and robustness, the Team will have identified all the process Xs (possible factors affecting performance) during the mapping in the Measure Phase.

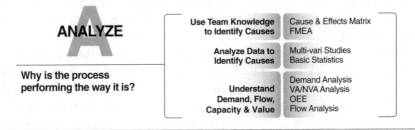

Figure 3.7 Analyze Phase roadmap

In this step, the Team uses slightly more subjective tools to narrow down the Xs to a more manageable number before the later, more intense data-driven tools are applied. A first rough cut is applied using a tool called a Cause and Effects (C&E) Matrix[5] to drop the Xs by approximately three-quarters. Then, a second, more detailed tool called a Failure Modes and Effects Analysis (FMEA)[6] is used to focus on the highest-risk Xs to reduce down to a final set of 10 to 15 primary Xs prior to applying the data-driven tools.

ANALYZE DATA TO IDENTIFY CAUSES

Data and data analyses are critical to Lean Sigma. Continuing with our accuracy/reliability-type problems, the Team uses an overarching data capture, planning, and analysis method called a multi-vari study, which involves more stringent statistical tools to objectively narrow down the Xs to the final few.

Data is captured for the remaining 10 to 15 Xs from the prior step and then analyzed graphically to identify any patterns or relationships, which are captured as potential hypotheses. For example, from Figure 3.8 we might identify the following potential hypotheses:

- Length of stay varies by ED physician.
- Variation in triage time is higher on the night shift.
- Wait time for a room varies by day of the week.
- Wait time is more variable on Saturdays, Tuesdays, and Thursdays.
- Length of stay in the ED is longer on the night shift than on the day shift.

Statistical analyses are then conducted on each of these potential hypotheses to identify which relationships are significant (real) and those for which the graphical hypotheses could have been exhibited purely by chance.[7] From the analytical results practical conclusions or implications are drawn as to the critical Xs and how they affect the performance of the process.

---

5. See Wedgwood, *Lean Sigma: A Practitioner's Guide*, pp. 153–57.

6. See Wedgwood, *Lean Sigma: A Practitioner's Guide*, pp. 325–29.

7. For a more detailed description of hypothesis testing, see Wedgwood, *Lean Sigma: A Practitioner's Guide*, pp. 300–305.

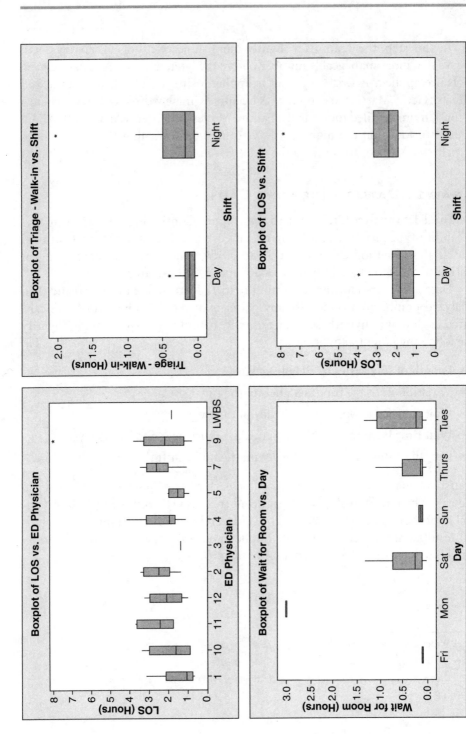

Figure 3.8 Graphical analysis of Xs during a multi-vari study

UNDERSTAND DEMAND, FLOW, CAPACITY, AND VALUE

For those projects and processes that are focused on capacity, throughput, flow, and timeliness (as opposed to accuracy and reliability), this step utilizes tools to understand the related issues and sources of waste or complexity hindering the ability of the process to meet performance requirements. The tools used are fairly disparate, but collectively they show the fundamental issues with the dynamics of the process.

IMPROVE

The purpose of Improve is to develop and implement the solution. Improve is the time when the solution(s) are finally constructed. Changes made in Lean Sigma are based on the data and understanding gained by this point in the project. The approach isn't to first decide on a solution, then commence a project to prove that it's the best solution and implement it.

Conceptual solutions are constructed based on the context of what has been learned from Define, Measure, and Analyze. Once a final concept is determined, the Team produces a detailed design and pilots the process to ensure its success. The steps and supporting tools for Improve are shown in Figure 3.9.

In the early days of Six Sigma in other (manufacturing) industries, solutions tended to relate to a simple change to an X in the process. Also in those other industries, the process had likely been designed at one time by a process engineer and hence was reasonably "clean." In healthcare, processes are rarely engineered from the beginning. More typically, they have evolved over time and are for the most part pretty messy. In other industries, there is also a predominance

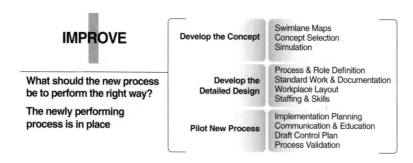

Figure 3.9 Improve Phase roadmap

of physical plant and equipment, whereas in healthcare, as in most other service industries, the predominant process "equipment" is human.

What these two factors mean in practice is that change in healthcare processes needs first, to include cleaning the whole process pretty much as a matter of course, and second, to involve the trickier scenario of changing people. When implementing change in this kind of environment, it's worth noting the three key requirements for an individual to be motivated to change:

1. I know *why* I'm being asked to change.
2. I know *what* is expected of me in the new process.
3. I feel *safe* doing it.

The Belt and Team will handle item 2 in developing the new process, constructing an implementation and education plan, but it is critical that leaders, including Champions and Process Owners, own items 1 and 3. From the outset of the project, leaders should be open about the business need for the project and associated process and role changes. They should also encourage the staff in feeling comfortable about their ability to perform their duties in light of any changes and be clear that staff will be supported throughout the transition.

DEVELOP THE CONCEPT

Lean Sigma is a highly innovative approach at this point in the roadmap. Rather than implementing a preconceived solution that tackles perhaps a small part of the process, the Team invariably considers the whole process from its fundamentals. Based on the context gained from the first three phases, innovation tools are used to generate a multitude of potential solutions, and these are tested against the process requirements. Components of the best solutions are hybridized together to form the new concept.

Once a new concept has been developed, there is an important project gate, at which point the key stakeholders sign off on the chosen solution. One common mistake made at this gate is that the leaders try to "cherry-pick" components that they like from the solution and deselect elements they don't like. This can be extremely detrimental for a couple of reasons:

1. Most solutions tend to be a holistic answer to the problem, and hence deselecting certain elements can unravel the solution to the point of being ineffective.

2. Deconstructing the solution conveys a message to the Team that their solution isn't trusted, which the Team can translate into "The leaders don't trust us. If they were just going to implement their answer, why did we go through all of this?"

As a leader it's important to remember that the best solution is the one that gets implemented and actually sticks. Remember that from the leadership position you don't often get the best view of how the work is done and how it might be done better.

A key activity once the concept is developed is to simulate the process and then to attempt to break it. The Team tries to identify scenarios that will cause the process to fail, with the intent of making it yet more robust. A useful tool here is to conduct a prospective risk analysis of the new process. The Team looks at new steps introduced into the process and brainstorms what might go wrong, how bad it would be, and how it can be mitigated. This will help the Team anticipate potential failures as they simulate the new process. Once the Team has tried this, they should engage key stakeholders, including Champions and Process Owners, to attempt the same.

DEVELOP THE DETAILED DESIGN

Once the concept has been agreed upon and signed off, it's only now worthwhile to spend Team time putting together the details of the process, the standard work, and the implementation plan.

The Team progresses systematically to

1. Add clarity to the process steps (definition, order, balance, pace, work sequence, flow)
2. Identify simple triggers to ensure uninterrupted flow of the process
3. Determine roles and accountability through the process to ensure clear ownership and balance of work content
4. Create Standard Work Instructions showing both the overarching flow of the process, but also fine detailed steps where needed
5. Lay out the workplace to support the process flow and the work conducted there
6. Ensure that competency is clearly defined for each role and thus create linkage to orientation and ongoing education

Once the process detail is created, the Team works to create a detailed implementation, communication, and education plan to be able to confidently deploy the new solution.

PILOT/RAMP UP THE NEW PROCESS

In many circumstances it's useful to pilot the new process prior to undertaking full-scale implementation. This is usually most relevant when the process is to be rolled out across multiple units or locations.

The term *pilot* has certain connotations, and here again is a difference in Lean Sigma from traditional approaches. Typically, piloting implies a test of a solution to see if it "fits." Once the pilot is complete, a decision might be made as to whether or not to commit to the solution. This approach can create problems with buy-in. "If we just wait this out and don't commit to it, we'll be back to our old approach in no time."

Here, piloting refers to the period during which the process is fine-tuned in situ. The new process is fully committed to before the pilot; the pilot just optimizes the solution. By taking this approach, the staff has to engage with the new process, because this is the only handholding they will get. "This new process is here to stay, so I need to understand it as soon as I can."

CONTROL

Once the new streamlined process is in place, the critical control elements are added to ensure that the process and hence its performance never revert to their original state. Once the Control Plan, as it is known, is in place, a second measure is conducted on the primary process performance metrics to ensure that the gains are real. Any gains are validated by the finance group. The steps and supporting tools for Control are shown in Figure 3.10.

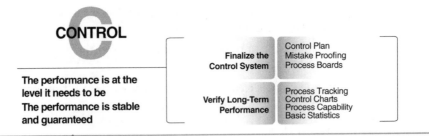

Figure 3.10 Control Phase roadmap

FINALIZE THE CONTROL SYSTEM

The Control Phase is a major difference between traditional approaches and Lean Sigma. The Control Plan is the complete package of physical changes, tools, documentation, measures, roles, and responsibilities that define the process in its new form.

The Control Plan in effect relies on, or can be considered to be part of, what is known as (process) performance management. The Control Plan Summary document captures the key decision points in the process where performance is managed. For example, consider a practical situation that targeted a registration process.[8] A key performance criterion for such a process is that patients get through the process in a timely manner. Patients wait ahead of a bank of four registration booths. At most times of day only two booths out of the four are needed to handle the volume of patient demand. However, at certain unpredictable times, spikes in demand occur and cause backlog at the two open booths, thus causing all new patients entering the process to wait for an unacceptable duration. To manage performance of the process, if patients wait for more than 10 minutes, phone registrars working adjacent to the booths are alerted and shift position temporarily, opening another booth to work down the backlog. Once it is cleared, they return to their original duties.

This localized performance management is reinforced by the manager but isn't overseen by anyone but the registrars themselves. The key metric of patient wait time is part of their daily scorecard, which they passionately drive.

VERIFY LONG-TERM PERFORMANCE

Once the Control Plan is in place, a second measure is conducted on the primary process performance metrics, and statistics are used to ensure that the gains are real (a statistically significant difference from the process performance before the project to after it). The gains are then validated by the finance group and entered into the program tracking documents.

THE LEAN SIGMA ROADMAP: WHY IT WORKS

At first glance the roadmap should seem just commonsense and straightforward, but it has a number of perhaps not-so-obvious built-in strengths, including at least

- Integral change management techniques
- Flexibility of approach to different problem types

---

8. Discussed in more detail in Case 6 in Chapter 4.

- Focus on customer need
- The right metrics to reduce complexity
- Goals set in a meaningful way
- Decisions based on the right data, not subjectivity
- Changes made in context
- Breakthrough change, not incremental improvement
- Changes locked in to assure that gains are maintained forever

INTEGRAL CHANGE MANAGEMENT TECHNIQUES

The people aspects of change are notoriously difficult to navigate and have spawned a plethora of techniques and approaches to ensure that change is implemented successfully and sustained. The Lean Sigma roadmap has multiple techniques built into it in a meaningful order, not limited to the following:

- There are mechanisms to ensure that throughout the project all parties are on the same page with respect to the project scope, purpose, measures, and solution.
- Key stakeholders (staff, managers, physicians, customers, etc.) are managed from problem to implemented solution.
- Solutions are based on data and the context of understanding gained along the way.
- A full complement of the right people closest to the process solve the problem.
- Composite solutions are developed, engaging all parties involved.
- Solutions are openly reviewed for critique and honing.
- Goal-driven project management methods underpin the roadmap.
- A systematic roadmap ensures that all parties know what's happening now, what's next, and why.
- Goals are set based on entitlement, to engage and drive thinking.
- Projects are resourced to a meaningful degree.
- Recipients of change understand the need for change, the newly developed solution, how they got there, their role in the solution, and what's expected of them.

FLEXIBILITY OF APPROACH TO DIFFERENT PROBLEM TYPES

Different business problems, depending on complexity and inherent difficulty of resolution, require different levels of rigor. The split-level roadmap with the higher-level goals (Initiate the Project, Define the Process, etc.), underpinned by flexible use of many available tools, allows latitude to tackle simple problems quickly and efficiently, while allowing higher degrees of rigor for more complex problems that require it. The roadmap is flexible so that it can be executed in a single event or spread across many shorter meetings, affording choice about how to manage resources within a project and across the program.

FOCUS ON CUSTOMER NEED

To determine the deliverables for the process, the Team could just accept the conventional thinking of what the process generates. Experience shows, however, that most processes are misunderstood, and in fact large pieces of processes often exist to deliver things that aren't truly needed by the customers of the process. Moreover, the true customers aren't often identified or consulted on what is needed from the process. The Team assumes it knows what the customer needs. Most often, it does not. The roadmap includes a series of tools to identify the customers, gather the VOC, distill it into a usable form, determine the major metrics and goals for the process, and derive a solution that meets these goals.

THE RIGHT METRICS TO REDUCE COMPLEXITY

The approach used doesn't tackle a single metric and try to improve it. Agreed, there may be one key metric related to the process that is giving the greatest pain, but it's important to consider all of the key metrics related to the process. The reason for this is best illustrated by using an example such as the case study on Medication Delivery in Chapter 4. Typically, projects related to this problem focus on just the accuracy of this particular process and not the timeliness of delivery. By focusing just on accuracy, the solution invariably involves adding some extra policing steps to the process—that is, we add more work to make things right. We patch the process. Each time someone examines the process, additional patches are added and the process complexity increases. As the complexity increases, so too does the risk of error (since it is more difficult to do the process), which is completely contrary to the objective. The better approach is to strip the process down to its fundamental pieces, remove all the complexity, and really focus on the essence of the process. A great tenet here is that if a step is designed out, that step can no longer be done wrong.

Our seemingly advanced systems have added much unneeded complexity, and our solutions often are driving in entirely the wrong direction, to add yet more complexity.

By considering all the key process metrics in the project and thus including the metric of timeliness of delivery in the objectives of the project, the focus is on doing things more quickly. To achieve this, the best approach is to remove unnecessary work from the process and streamline it. Simpler, streamlined processes tend to be much easier to do and are more consistently applied and thus more reliable.

GOALS SET IN A MEANINGFUL WAY

If goals are set based on entitlement, they are completely achievable from a Lean Sigma standpoint but are much greater than what could be achieved by other means. The stretch nature of the goal engages the Team and moves them well beyond the realm of just making minor tweaks. Once the project is complete, such magnitude of change is less prone to be overwritten by future tweaking and is thus more likely to be sustained.

DECISIONS BASED ON THE RIGHT DATA, NOT SUBJECTIVITY

In most healthcare organizations there is an abundance of data but very little information. Lean Sigma seeks to base decisions and changes on reliable data, thus removing subjectivity. "We're making a particular change because that's what the data shows us."

CHANGES MADE IN CONTEXT

Changes made in Lean Sigma are based on the learning and understanding gained prior to the Improve Phase. The approach isn't to first decide on a solution, then commence a project to prove that's the best solution and implement it. Instead, based on the context gained from the first three phases, innovation tools are used to combine smaller components of solutions to form the new concept. The Team then forms the detailed design of the process around the agreed-upon concept.

BREAKTHROUGH CHANGE, NOT INCREMENTAL IMPROVEMENT

As described in Chapter 1, the more traditional performance improvement methods used in healthcare rely on the notion of continuous improvement and thus drive continuous change in processes, hence causing a constant churn and inevitably leading to degraded performance.

Lean Sigma, with its breakthrough change approach, not only drives bigger change over a shorter time frame but also, because staff are not required to subsequently continuously improve the process, ensures that gains are more likely to be sustained.

CHANGES LOCKED IN TO ASSURE THAT GAINS ARE MAINTAINED FOREVER

Changes made using traditional performance improvement methods typically fail to sustain, due to the many reasons described in Chapter 1.

However, once changes have been effected in Lean Sigma, the strong emphasis on control methods in the latter stages of the roadmap, including Standard Work Instructions and the Control Plan, ensure that subsequent performance is managed and maintained.

STANDARDIZATION PROJECTS

For many processes the issue is that staff all do the process somewhat differently. Substantial change isn't necessarily required. The need is more to define what the standard process should be (say what we do), and then have everyone follow it, every time (do what we say).

The recommended approach is shown in Figure 3.11. The approach has two main threads: one related to defining the standard process, the second to following it.

Figure 3.11 Flow of standardization projects

To define the process, a short standardization event is used. Prior to the event, preparation work is done to ensure that the event goes off smoothly, and once the event is complete, there is usually some degree of follow-on implementation and education.

The roadmap used is a cut-down version of the full DMAIC change roadmap adapted specifically for standardization. Rather than incorporating an Improve Phase, because no significant change is being made, a replacement Standardization Phase is used, thus creating the new DMASC roadmap. The major steps in the roadmap are very similar to those of DMAIC, and the tools used represent a small subset of the DMAIC tools portfolio. The full three-layer roadmap is shown in Figure 3.12.

To complete the full roadmap in the shortened time frame, a few corners are cut as follows:

- *Determine Customer Requirements becomes Review Customer Requirements.* No extensive VOC work is conducted. The Team reviews the purpose of the process, as it is currently understood.

- *Develop & Evaluate Measurement Systems* is removed. If the process capability is initially unknown (the process performance isn't measured), the Team continues regardless. During the Control Phase appropriate measures are put into place, so subsequent performance is tracked.

- *Analyze Data to Identify Causes* is removed. Detailed statistics are avoided. The purpose of DMASC is not to identify the root cause of low performance and then change; it is simply to standardize to what should be an already understood process, so the detail of this step is not needed.

- *Develop the Concept* is substantially lessened, since the complexity of evolving a wholly new process is avoided.

- Implementation typically is much smoother and less intensive, since the standard process by definition is relatively well understood.

Based on this fairly extensive list of omissions, many might question the point of such an endeavor. What is striking is the magnitude of change in the performance based on the approach. In a recent rollout across 42 major hospital processes, approximately one-third had not had performance measured before, so no insight could be gained into the magnitude of the improvement. However, the remaining two-thirds all saw an expected reduction in variability in performance. What was surprising was that about half of those processes also saw a significant shift in the mean of the process (defects reduced, cycle times reduced, etc.), and many showed hard-dollar savings.

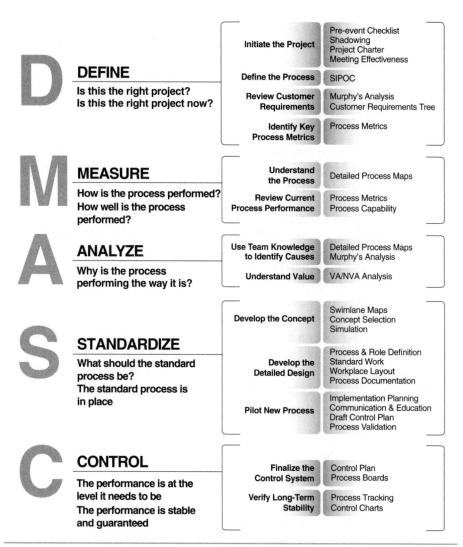

Figure 3.12 Standardization roadmap

KAIZEN (ACCELERATED CHANGE) EVENTS

Accelerated change events, often known as Kaizen events, are frequently used within a Lean Sigma program. It is possible to conduct such an event outside of a program, but the focus here is on leading within a Lean Sigma environment, so we'll not consider that possibility further.

A (Lean Sigma) Kaizen event is a means for effecting change very quickly, in a matter of days versus weeks, but for a very specific problem set. Let's reiterate that last statement: *for a very specific problem set.* This approach is applicable for projects that

- Don't require extensive analytics and data capture
- Aren't focused on accuracy or defects
- Instead focus on streamlining, improving flow, or removing complexity and thus increasing capacity or throughput or reducing cycle time and length of time through the process (e.g., length of stay)

The work is achieved through use of a team-based event, typically of four or five days, depending on the complexity of the process. The roadmap is shown in Figure 3.13.

To ensure that the event is efficient and effective, some prework is needed on the part of the event leader, Champion, and Process Owner. The event is chartered in the same manner as a Lean Sigma project. The event leader shadows in the area to gain an understanding of the process, language, and so on. Relevant data is captured and analyzed offline, typically related to demand, capacity, lead times (e.g., length of stay), and cycle times. A baseline is established, plus an understanding gained for the primary process delays and losses in capacity.

The daily event activity follows the Figure 3.13 roadmap steps approximately as follows:

- Day 1: Current state
  - Understand the process
  - Understand demand, flow, capacity, and value
- Day 2: Develop the future state
  - Develop the concept and sign off
  - Develop the detailed design
- Days 3–5: Implement and stabilize the new process

The work across days 3 to 5 can vary, depending on the magnitude of the rollout. If the change is localized to a small department, or is across a small number of staff, the process can be implemented on day 3, stabilized, and a Control Plan developed. If, however, the number of staff involved in the process is too large to effect change successfully during the event without a high degree of risk, the Team makes all the possible (smaller) changes they can and then focuses the

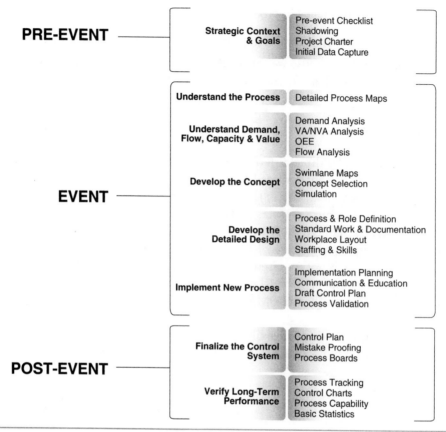

Figure 3.13 Lean Sigma Kaizen roadmap

remainder of the time planning the rollout and go-live for a time beyond the event itself. This allows a certain degree of flexibility and ensures that the Team can drive as much change as possible in a short time frame, without either stalling out or attempting anything too far-reaching or risky without the appropriate planning and diligence.

A well-run Kaizen looks remarkably easy to facilitate, but in fact the approach requires a very high degree of skill and experience in the facilitator. These types of events can yield remarkable results very quickly but if not well planned and led can fizzle out just as easily.

Building Post-Event activity into the roadmap ensures that the control system is finalized, implementation is complete, and performance is verified.

As with any shortened approach, the biggest pitfalls are

1. Trying to apply the method to problems outside of the list of applicability
2. Assuming that because we can accelerate things to 4 to 5 days, we must be able to squeeze them further to (say) 2 to 3 days

SUMMARY

Lean Sigma provides three different roadmaps, each one applicable to a variety of problem scenarios encountered.

The most generic of these, the DMAIC roadmap, is applicable across the majority of improvement projects that involve changing the process. For a subset of these projects, namely, those limited to changes focused on flow and streamlining, the simpler, accelerated Kaizen roadmap is useful. For projects where significant change is not required and the problem relates more to the fact that different staff members involved in the various steps of the process perform the process steps differently, the DMASC process standardization roadmap is very effective.

Each roadmap is simple, flexible, and goal-driven. All have critical thinking embedded within them, to aid in navigation from problem to solution.

APPLICATION TO REAL LIFE

Project Case Examples

The list of projects conducted in healthcare using Lean Sigma methods likely touches virtually all aspects of the business. Here, the focus is on the leaders' learning, and so the selected case examples reflect both different problem types, but also different Lean Sigma approaches. For each example, attention is focused not so much on the solution itself, but rather on the characteristics of the business situation and the path used to get to the solution.

The cases appear in approximate order of complexity of approach.

CASE 1: CT CAPACITY AND THROUGHPUT

BACKGROUND/SITUATION

A hospital's radiology department includes a computed tomography (CT) department with two scanners, conducting approximately 750 scans per month. The hospital was experiencing decreasing volume and losing associated revenue to a freestanding competitor. Initial Voice of the Customer (VOC) work had indicated that much of the volume loss was due to the hospital requiring that patients schedule tests in advance (on average more than two days), whereas the competitor accepted walk-ins. Some same-day scans were feasible, but the process was convoluted and difficult for both the patient and the department.

In its baseline state, both inpatients and outpatients (ED and scheduled ambulatory patients) were distributed across both scanners, and all staff played all roles, with no real clarity of who owned what at any time. Both scanners were considered to be at, or nearing, maximum capacity.

The focus of the project was to increase the CT capacity, create greater access for patients, and recoup as much lost patient demand as possible.

APPROACH

Given that the CT department was relatively small and the project urgency was very high, the usual Lean Sigma or Kaizen approaches (as described in Chapter 3) were not attractive options. The organization elected to do the majority of the solution concept design in a single two-day Kaizen-type event, led by the author in the role of Master Black Belt.

The choice to use an external resource mainly related to the inexperience of the Black Belt leading the project. Given the criticality of the outcome to the organization, use of a seasoned resource was deemed a better prospect for success.

Prior to the event, three or four one-hour team meetings were conducted over a period of about a month to charter and prepare the work and to plan, capture, and analyze data related to demand, cycle times, staffing, and VOC. Many of the flow changes were made during the two-day event, but some long-lead-time items, such as changes to staffing levels and staff competence, were managed through a series of meetings after the event, over a two-week period. The overarching project timeline is shown in Figure 4.1.

Figure 4.1 High-level phases of CT Capacity and Throughput project

CHANGES MADE

The majority of the improvement came from reducing the lost room capacity due to pre- and post-exam work being conducted in the scanner room. Before the event, there was activity in the exam room that didn't need to occur there. For example, patient histories were taken pre-exam, and patient instructions were given post-exam. Both activities are important but can be done outside the exam room. In addition, clear, simple, repeatable, and singly accountable roles ensured no lost time due to "do-overs" or missed activity.

The increase in capacity allowed all the outpatient "runners" to be put on the single fastest scanner, thus freeing up the second scanner for inpatient work and longer procedures, further reducing delays due to the scanners being tied up simultaneously.

RESULTS

The capacity increase was significant (the Overall Equipment Effectiveness[1] was increased five-fold) with a corresponding reduction in outpatient turnaround time from 23 minutes to less than 10 minutes. This enabled the department to accept walk-ins, thus recapturing substantial volume from the freestanding competitor.

Within a matter of weeks volume was up 30% with a corresponding 38% increase in revenue. Spreading the fixed overhead of the department across many more scans significantly improved margins.

LEADERSHIP LEARNING

Such a simple project has many learning points for leaders:

1. Within a small department it's possible to change the project structure to cater for reduced availability of team members.

2. It's often useful to apply external resources as Project Leaders when internal resource bandwidth or capability is limited and when rapid change is required.

---

1. Overall Equipment Effectiveness (OEE) in Lean Sigma is an analogous but more sophisticated measure of utilization and relates actual capacity to potential capacity. In simple terms, a process running at 100% OEE is up 100% of the time, doing only value-added work, is going as fast as it has ever gone, and is running with perfect quality. See Wedgwood, *Lean Sigma: A Practitioner's Guide,* pp. 311–17.

3. For large opportunity projects touching the external market, it is recommended to conduct a VOC data capture and analysis to ensure that the focus of the project is most relevant.

4. Once a simple accountable set of roles is developed for a process, the system as a whole becomes very resilient and is sustained well (see the Epilogue for this case study).

5. It's possible to dramatically increase the capacity of a process, even when it has been considered to be "maxed out."

EPILOGUE

This particular project was completed in 2007. Some five years later the author met one of the Kaizen participants, a CT tech, in the cafeteria at the hospital. She was still excited about how well the process was running and volunteered to talk to other CT departments attempting the same goal (including the team described in Case 10). Her main message regarding why it was so successful related to how with simple accountability in place, there was, in her words, ". . . no longer any place for low performers to hide."

At that time the volume had increased drastically from the initial 750 scans per month, and the same process was now conducting on average around 1,300 scans per month.

CASE 2: REDUCE DISCHARGED, NOT FINAL BILLED (DNFB)

BACKGROUND/SITUATION

A hospital commenced its Lean Sigma journey and selected a variety of business targets for initial projects. One such target was the ability to quickly bill for services rendered. Net revenue of approximately $200 million and an average DNFB[2] of 11 days equated to more than $4 million outstanding unbilled at any time.

---

2. DNFB is defined as unbilled net revenue divided by average daily net revenue.

A DNFB of less than five days is a reasonable goal for most organizations, thus representing, in this case, a project opportunity of more than $2.5 million cash.

APPROACH

Given that DNFB was impacted by multiple sequential processes through the organization's Health Information and Patient Financial Services, the approach taken was first to conduct "discovery" work across a very broad scope of processes and then, based on the learning gained, focus the subsequent project work on the greatest source of opportunity, in this case the processing of paper charts in Health Information.

Once the Health Information focus was determined, the project followed the typical Lean Sigma roadmap as described in Chapter 3.

CHANGES MADE

Scanning, or imaging, paper documents into an electronic record archive constituted a significant activity in the DNFB process. Instead of segmenting the imaging process by activity and working with batches of charts at each phase, the team organized a single-piece flow. Two methods of chart flow were instigated; either a single person or a pair of staff managed each chart through the entire process. Work patterns were established, along with workstations and layouts that met physical needs. Staffing patterns were changed to match chart volume.

RESULTS

After the introduction of the changes, results were dramatic. As shown in Figure 4.2, the time required to prepare, scan, and review a chart declined from an average of around 11 hours to less than 1. Equally important to staff is that now it is rare that one shift leaves work undone for the next shift, and when they do, it is quickly completed.

DNFB days dropped from an average of 11 days to a sustained rate averaging 5 days. At the same time, the hospital brought a one-time increase of nearly $2.5 million in revenues to its bottom line, as verified by the chief financial officer. Also, the Team enabled staff to improve the time when charts are available for clinical and operational reviews, updates, or readmissions.

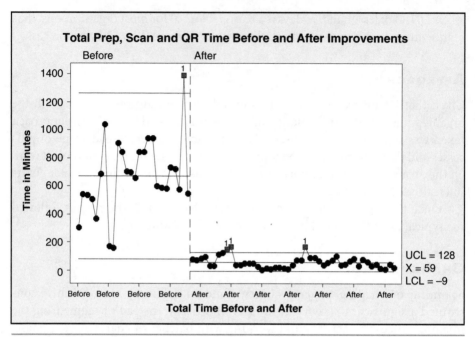

Figure 4.2 Reduction in processing time in Health Information

LEADERSHIP LEARNING

Key leadership learning points for this project include the following:

1. Focus on cash processes is good for quick return, especially in the early stages of a Lean Sigma deployment. Once the process change is made, the cash shift can be realized in as little as a few weeks (unlike profitability change projects, which can take months or even years to make a similar impact).

2. When the specific failing process is unknown, it's prudent to scope the project broadly initially (with a "discovery" thinking) and then scope down later once the target process has been determined.

3. It is very common that, on hearing of an impending project in their area, operations leaders (Process Owners) try to solve the problem independently, often by throwing resources at it, with no real change to the process. Figure 4.3 shows this initial attempt (labeled "Special Cause"), after which the process performance reverts to its baseline.

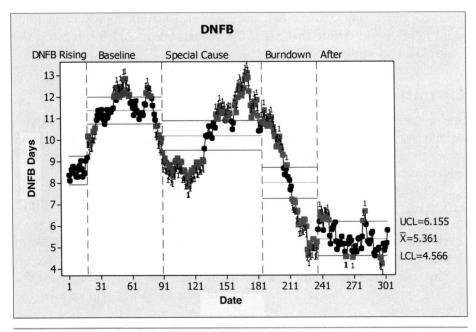

Figure 4.3 DNFB performance over time

CASE 3: RADIOLOGY DENIALS

BACKGROUND/SITUATION

A medium-size regional health system, given the financial tightening during healthcare reform, was looking at all process opportunities for reducing costs. The internal Revenue Integrity Team had identified a potential issue with payer denials in radiology.

Prior-year data showed denials of approximately $660,000 with a similar run rate in the current year. The situation was complicated further by a number of physician office changes under way to ensure that revenue was secured for the health system and not diverted elsewhere.

APPROACH

Given the magnitude of the existing performance improvement under way, the Lean Sigma Steering Team elected to use the author as an external resource to lead an initial Kaizen event to design the new process and implement where possible. Subsequent to the event, internal performance improvement leads could follow up to ensure that all of the changes were implemented and the Control Plan was fully functional.

CHANGES MADE

During the event, it became very obvious that the process was overly complex, with no clear ownership at any stage. More staff were being used to inspect and rework the patient accounts than were doing the work in the first place. A simple process with clear accountabilities was developed.

Second, the complex pre-authorization work was falling on multiple lesser-trained individuals in the physician offices, rather than on the higher-skilled resources (currently focused on the inspection and rework). The simple tenet of "Do it with the right skilled person, right the first time" drove the team to a model of using revenue cycle experts to do the authorizations and free up the physician office staff to focus on scheduling and registration and easing the patients' journey to the next point of care. This was a win-win-win for all of the involved parties.

RESULTS

Since the implementation of the changes, the denials were reduced by more than 50%. In addition, by simplifying the process for physician offices, the changes caused a few key physicians to reconsider their stance of using an external competitor for their CTs. The hospital subsequently captured some 250 additional cases per month in CT.

The bigger impact, however, was that this event helped the leadership to recognize the potential in the revenue cycle and to subsequently launch a program to simplify and strengthen processes across the breadth of the revenue cycle.

LEADERSHIP LEARNING

Key learning points for leaders are as follows:

1. Sometimes it's important to spend a little extra to get a project done now, rather than wait until internal resources are available. If the organization is losing significant money every month, it's important to consider the opportunity cost of not doing the project, which can outweigh the additional investment in external resources to lead the project.

2. External benchmarks can be useful to identify potential project opportunities but should not prevent a project from being tackled. If this particular organization had gone by benchmark alone, it wouldn't have commenced the project at all, but the raw level of denials at $660,000 per year (much less than the $3 million benchmark best practice) couldn't be ignored.

3. Involving and engaging the right people, both on the Team but also as Champions and Process Owners, is critical. For some reason, organizations default to a single project Champion, when in reality two or even more are required to bring about the change.

4. In more recent times, the avoidance of adding staff to gain a desired return is almost at paranoia level. Too many times, organizations are losing out on multiple times return on investment (ROI) because they don't want to add a required full-time position. There has also been a preponderance of cutting heads in the wrong place (at the front lines) and then adding them back in the wrong place (service line directors) when performance inevitably drops. A great tenet here is to simplify, add the right resource where it is needed, empower the front line, and manage performance.

CASE 4: BEHAVIORAL HEALTH DISCOVERY

BACKGROUND/SITUATION

A large not-for-profit provider of community-based behavioral healthcare had seen a key performance indicator for patient satisfaction well below benchmark for some time, to the point of impacting remuneration. The patient group in question was adolescents (the patient satisfaction surveys were actually being filled out by the parents, not the patients themselves).

Many changes had been attempted, but nothing seemed to move the performance. The organization took advantage of a local hospital Black Belt training wave and added three key leaders to take the training, with this particular project being one of the three chosen for focus during training.

APPROACH

Given the absolute lack of data and understanding of why the patient satisfaction was so low, the chosen project path was one of discovery, specifically of the VOC. In effect, the project followed Define-Measure-Analyze and then spawned a number of actions and subsequent projects based on the new customer insight.

CHANGES MADE

Based on the VOC work, there were a number of subsequent areas of activity, the two most notable being these:

1. They were measuring patient satisfaction differently from the organizations to which they were being compared. Simply resetting the measurement to match standard helped greatly.
2. Some earlier changes such as the removal of provision of transport as a cost-cutting measure (which was deemed unnecessary) had in fact had a very marked negative ramification.

RESULTS

The largest positive result here was likely the big step forward in understanding customer need. Based on simple changes based on the VOC work, patient satisfaction was elevated to new levels that were higher than had ever been experienced in the past.

LEADERSHIP LEARNING

Key leadership learning from the project is as follows:

1. A great place to look for Lean Sigma projects in the organization is where performance is still low despite multiple attempts to remedy the situation. Often these are avoided because of a concern that there is limited value or there perhaps isn't a high chance of success.
2. Being brave enough to admit that "we don't know" was tough for leadership, but committing to an open-ended VOC activity brought significant return.
3. Sometimes one project isn't a single project but in fact spawns many others. Sometimes the project we're working on now is merely an enabler.

CASE 5: MEDICATION DELIVERY

BACKGROUND/SITUATION

A medium-size regional hospital in the initial stages of a Lean Sigma deployment had selected four Black Belts to be trained and a spread of projects across the organization to learn what Lean Sigma could accomplish. A competitor hospital had recently had an adverse event due to a medication error, and most hospitals in the region had heightened sensitivity to the issue. An earlier isolated project had examined medication administration, and this project was a continuation of that work.

APPROACH

The project was scoped to just first-dose delivery to inpatient units, from order written to medication available to nurse for administration. Initial data captured indicated an accuracy rate at around 93.5% for getting the medication to the nursing unit with the "five rights" (right med, right dose, right route, right patient, right time) and an average delivery time of 86 minutes.

The project followed the Lean Sigma project approach as described in Chapter 3, first streamlining the process and then giving heavy scrutiny to the accuracy and reliability of the delivery itself.

CHANGES MADE

Changes focused on two main areas: first, how meds were stored on the inpatient units, and second, the flow of the process to and through the pharmacy.

Current practice is often for hospital units to store medications in, and dispense them from, a medication vault that tracks the inventory. Historically, at this hospital, only controlled and a limited number of commonly used meds were stored on the unit in med vaults. The team elected to include all high-usage meds in the vaults to eliminate the lengthy and potentially unreliable process of delivery from the pharmacy.

The pharmacy flow was redesigned to give quiet, focused attention to order entry, rather than it being done in the hustle and bustle of the main pharmacy area.

Attention was paid to the layout of both the pharmacy itself and the med rooms on the inpatient units.

RESULTS

As a result, the hospital reduced average medication delivery time by 60% and improved accuracy of the first dispensed dose to just one error in greater than 18,000 opportunities, a thousand-fold reduction in errors.

In addition to the accuracy and timeliness, some unexpected results included more than $200,000 annually in recovered charges along with a 55% reduction in the number and 60% reduction in the length of phone calls between the nursing units and the pharmacy.

LEADERSHIP LEARNING

Key leadership learning for this project includes the following:

1. Results can come from multiple areas: timeliness and accuracy of med delivery, phone calls between inpatient units and the pharmacy, nurse interruptions, charge capture, work content of the process, reduction of paperwork in the process, and elimination of reconciliation of copies of paperwork where splits in the process have occurred.

2. Often healthcare processes are so messy that in order to increase accuracy, it's important to streamline the process substantially (the inherent quality of the process is a function of its complexity).

3. Many processes require more than one Champion to bring about success. Here it was necessary that both the director of nursing and the pharmacy director be Champions. Without either one, the project would likely not have succeeded.

CASE 6: REGISTRATION STANDARDIZATION

BACKGROUND/SITUATION

A medium-size regional hospital approximately six years into its Lean Sigma deployment, having completed more than 40 projects, was beginning to see patterns in sustainability of results. Where processes were clearly understood, repetitive, and with a relatively short cycle time, such as in pharmacy and lab, process improvements were well controlled and sustained. In other areas there were some struggles.

Discussion with executive leadership resulted in articulation of the problem as a lack of understanding of (process) performance management. An organization-wide initiative commenced to roll out process standardization and performance management. Each department was required to identify at least one core process to standardize.

Main registration was selected for the pilot work and was led by the author (an external resource) with the commonly used theme of "If we've not done this internally before, let's watch it being done right and we'll learn from that." (Case 7 was the subsequent, more complex event and followed the same thinking.)

Prior to the work, patient satisfaction with registration was at the 76th percentile.

APPROACH

The project followed the two parallel standardization paths, as described in Chapter 3 and depicted in Figure 3.11. The first path focused on the registration process itself. Through use of a two-day standardization event, the team laid down the standard process and created the Standard Work Instructions. During the event, a draft Control Plan Summary was developed.

The second path was aimed specifically at the frontline manager and supervisors in the area, guiding them in the project output they were being given, what it meant to have a standardized process, and how to manage performance.

CHANGES MADE

Since this was a standardization approach, some streamlining of the process was involved, but there was no substantial (new to the organization) change. There were many of the same process steps, but some were done in a slightly different order. In addition, the team applied workplace layout design principles to the registration booths and main registration area.

RESULTS

Subsequent to the event, patient satisfaction has risen from the baseline at the 76th percentile to consistently higher than the 95th percentile and has been sustained.

LEADERSHIP LEARNING

Leadership learning from this project includes the following:

1. Given that this was a first attempt at the new standardization approach, an external facilitator was used and the chosen target area was relatively small, self-contained, with an important and quickly cycling process.

2. Two distinct parallel paths were used: first, to say what we do, and second, to do what we say.

3. Staff quickly realized that performance management isn't about "big brother watching me" but relates closely to equitable distribution of workload. With this realization, the staff in the registration area asked to move from measuring staff productivity monthly to twice a shift.

4. Unlike a change project, it was important to include the Process Owner (registration manager) on the Team to ensure that the standard process was clearly understood and staff could be held accountable for it.

5. Building the requirement that managers standardize their processes into their annual performance appraisal quickly drove the culture of standard work into the organization. As shown in Figure 3.11, three audits were used: one to get a 3 on the scorecard (gained after completing the event), the second to get a 4 on the scorecard (gained once all standard tools were in place), and finally to get a 5 on the scorecard (gained with a presentation to the audit team).

EPILOGUE

Very quickly after go-live the manager became free of getting drawn down into the weeds of expediting patients and was able to get back to real managerial duties. She very much embraced the approaches and quickly moved the staff members to standardize all the other registration processes.

CASE 7: INPATIENT ADMISSION STANDARDIZATION

BACKGROUND/SITUATION

This case was conducted at the same organization as Case 6, as part of the standardization initiative. Once the initial registration pilot was complete, some reasonably small departmental processes were tackled, but when inpatient nursing was to be addressed (considered a higher-complexity and higher-risk undertaking), the same approach of using the author as an external facilitator for the event was used.

The admission assessment process was selected as being a core nursing process, with the notion that if it were done right, many potential failures/problems later in the process would not occur.

APPROACH

The same approach was used as shown in Figure 3.11 in a longer four-day standardization event. Representation from all nursing units was included in the event, as well as all nurse managers. Mentoring in performance management was given in parallel to nurse managers and supervisors.

CHANGES MADE

The Team concluded that most issues in the process could be avoided if the RN conducting the assessment was not interrupted. Even though this was a standardization event, the Team elected to make a change to the process and have the RNs hand off their phone to their second prior to the assessment.

The assessment itself was streamlined and sequenced for maximum efficiency.

RESULTS

The phone handoff proved to be a critical X (factor) in the process, driving out more than 40 minutes from the assessment duration, along with a reduction in variation; in other words, the work was done more consistently and more efficiently.

LEADERSHIP LEARNING

Leadership learning from this project includes the following:

1. When improving a lengthy process or sequence of processes, it's often good to start at the front to get things right the first time (everything flows from there).

2. If all nursing units are impacted, it's imperative to get all the managers in the room. If we are looking for one standardized process, there's really just one decision-making body.

3. It's often tough to get different units to buy in, even when data is presented. It takes constant reinforcement from leadership.

4. Building key process measures into a manager's scorecard will drive sustainability.

CASE 8: PHYSICIAN OFFICE STANDARDIZATION

BACKGROUND/SITUATION

In its effort to gain patient-centered medical home (PCMH)[3] recognition, a health system leveraged its long-term Lean Sigma program and experience of process standardization to meet the NCQA[4] requirements in an efficient and disciplined manner.

Based on commitments to local employers, the timeline to achieve accreditation across eight physician practices was a very short seven months.

APPROACH

With such a short time frame to contend with, a typical standardization approach for each process would have taken more than two years, so it was deemed inappropriate. Instead, the route taken was a hybrid program approach, as shown in Figure 4.4.

In Phase 1, process change, led by a Black Belt, was driven across all eight practices directly from updating policies to the new requirements. During this phase, auditing of compliance with requirements was tracked, and a list of projects was identified for needed improvement in Phase 2. Once the practices were compliant with the required levels, the NCQA application was submitted.

---

3. A team-based healthcare delivery model led by a primary care physician that provides comprehensive and continuous medical care to patients with the goal of obtaining maximized health outcomes.

4. The National Committee for Quality Assurance is an accrediting and standards-setting body for a number of healthcare-related organizations, including managed care and patient-centered medical homes.

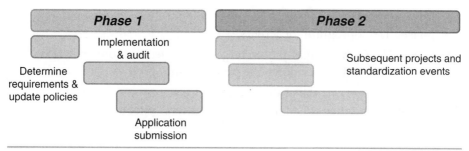

Figure 4.4 Phase approach to meeting NCQA requirements

CHANGES MADE

The changes implemented all related directly to the NCQA standards and included access to medical records, access to a physician, as well as callbacks and other preventive measures for key population groups.

RESULTS

All eight practices received recognition within the seven-month period, and seven out of the eight achieved the highest possible level. Based on the changes, appointment availability has increased significantly, and there has been a positive impact on preventive care related to callbacks for key areas such as mammography and colonoscopy.

LEADERSHIP LEARNING

Leadership learning from this project includes the following:

1. It was useful to see Lean Sigma as a tool to achieve strategic goals, for example, meeting NCQA accreditation and Meaningful Use.[5]
2. Lean Sigma Black Belts become very strong Project Leaders and are highly suitable for this kind of endeavor even though the approach was not classical Lean Sigma.

---

5. The Medicare and Medicaid electronic health record (EHR) Incentive Programs provide financial incentives for the meaningful use of certified EHR technology to improve patient care.

3. It was important to approach the issue not as a single project, but as a phased Tier 2 program[6] of activity.

4. Standardization was useful once targets were met, to shore up performance gaps and to lock down the processes more fully.

5. Rather than solving the problems one office at a time, the solution was built once and then rolled out to all offices in a "pilot and proliferate" fashion.

CASE 9: SURGERY CAPACITY AND THROUGHPUT

BACKGROUND/SITUATION

A hospital's main surgery was experiencing difficulties with on-time starts and throughput and had a substantial backlog in demand. Key surgeon groups were expressing frustration at not being able to get block[7] or even schedule time and had indicated that their dissatisfaction might force them to conduct their procedures at other facilities.

APPROACH

To make a large enough change in short order, leadership elected to mobilize four Kaizen events run in parallel, scrutinizing each of the areas of patient intake, in-OR activity, post-surgery care, and OR room turns. Surgery leaders had heard of the Kaizen approach and felt it was an appropriate one, but the organization, early in its Lean Sigma deployment, hadn't had any experience with leading such events.

This was a huge endeavor involving some 53 team members, Champions, and Process Owners, and each event was led by a separate (external) facilitator.

Prior to the events, preparation was done across all four events, first as a group and then with each event Team separately. Once the events were complete, a three-month rollout plan commenced to take, for example, learning from one room turnover type to other types in order of frequency (see Figure 4.5).

---

6. Please see Chapter 2, "Project Tiers."

7. Regular scheduled time set aside for a surgeon or surgery group.

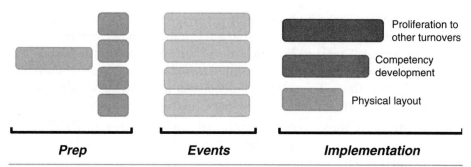

Figure 4.5 Surgery Capacity and Throughput project timeline

CHANGES MADE

Given that this was in effect just a very large Kaizen event, the sheer number of changes was large, but the level of sophistication was low—in Lean Sigma vernacular, "low tech, high touch," but a lot of it. Most activity focused on basic flow and streamlining of the processes.

RESULTS

Key turnover times were reduced substantially, for example, for going from one major case type to a different major case type; room turnover time was reduced from 42 minutes to 14 minutes.

The bigger result was that three key surgeons who had been threatening to leave stayed and the surgery protected its revenue base.

LEADERSHIP LEARNING

Leadership learning from this project includes the following:

1. Four events in parallel required senior executive-level commitment, a surgeon in every event, plus the chief of staff and anesthesiology floating among events.

2. Such longitudinal change often creates very high levels of stress (everyone's cheese was moved at once), but even the simplest change management techniques pay dividends in such an environment.

3. To ensure that everyone was on the same page throughout the events, daily calibration meetings occurred across the events at the start of the day, at lunch, and at the end of each day.

4. As is common early in a Lean Sigma deployment, there was no performance management in place, and so it was initially tough to maintain performance. There was little in terms of basic operational thinking (solutions up to this point had mainly focused on just increasing staffing and fighting fires). The director and manager regularly spoke of being "hands-on" with much talk of needing a "high-performing team."

5. Unfortunately, the surgery director baked in a lot of other unrelated solutions under the banner of the Kaizen work, which required a certain amount of damage control later.

EPILOGUE

The surgery director was subsequently "freed up to develop her career potential elsewhere." The new director was very focused on operations management, visibility, and clarity of roles. With such stronger performance management, much of the benefit of the events only really came to fruition under the new culture; turnaround times met those demonstrated during the events, and the surgery volume increased.

CASE 10: EMERGENCY DEPARTMENT THROUGHPUT

BACKGROUND/SITUATION

A medium-large health system had a large hospital-based ED with 50+ rooms catering to more than 80,000 visits per year. The department had long had patient satisfaction issues with long average length of stay and subsequently many patients being seen in the lobby area. ED leadership was considering spending substantial capital to revamp the lobby area to create additional treatment rooms but instead opted for a performance improvement effort first.

APPROACH

The endeavor was structured as a Tier 2 program of multiple sequenced events and projects. Given the complexity of the undertaking and multiple departments involved, a Steering Group was formed composed of all ancillary directors, ED leadership, finance, and ED physician leadership. The Steering Group championed the program as a whole and performed early work to identify the core processes and baseline performance. An initial assessment or "discovery" helped the Steering Group determine which core processes to tackle and in what order.

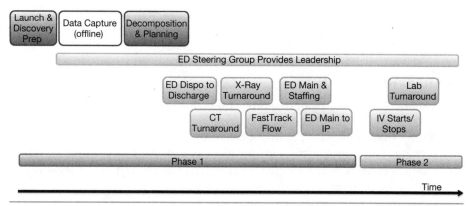

Figure 4.6 Emergency Department Throughput program timeline

The first phase of the work, conducted over six months as shown in Figure 4.6, targeted six major ED processes, each one with an appropriately scoped Kaizen event. Subsequent phases included additional events, plus Lean Sigma projects.

CHANGES MADE

Each Phase 1 Kaizen focused on streamlining a core ED process, determined the best operating models to maximize capacity of supporting ancillary areas, and laid down clear role accountability.

One large event tackled the main ED operational (staffing) model as well as the primary ED flow.

Simple changes, such as those described in Case 1, allowed, for example, an ED-CT-focused event to create much increased CT capacity and so reduce ED-CT turnaround time.

RESULTS

Phase 1 results were very encouraging:

1. The number of patients being seen in the lobby was reduced from 21% to 0%.
2. Patient satisfaction increased from the initial 15th percentile up to the 91st percentile.
3. ED-CT turnaround time was down more than 40%.

4. General X-ray turnaround time was down more than 40%.

5. ED-inpatient admit time was down 50%.

LEADERSHIP LEARNING

Key leadership learning from this program includes the following:

1. Rather than conducting multiple (seemingly unconnected) events or projects, it is better to approach the problem as a simple Tier 2 program. That way it becomes easier for departmental staff and the rest of the organization to understand and connect with the work.

2. It's often useful to take a whole "value stream" approach rather than just focusing on (in this case) the ED. Key connected ancillary processes, such as imaging, are integral to the ED performance.

3. In such a complex environment, it's very useful to set up a Steering Group, comprising all key leaders and physicians, to guide the program. The Steering Group continues to meet to guide overarching ED performance improvement and ensure that the ED meets scorecard and strategic goals.

4. It's helpful to phase the work in meaningful sections so it doesn't appear to be a never-ending effort.

5. All Phase 1 work was facilitated by an external resource, and internal capability was ramped up and used exclusively in Phase 2.

6. Almost constant communication was vital and included progress, success to date, and upcoming activities.

CASE II: INPATIENT PLACEMENT

BACKGROUND/SITUATION

With the advent of shifting patient population away from inpatient, a hospital was experiencing reduced volumes and utilization on its inpatient units, subsequent difficulties in staffing, and hence low and even negative margins for many DRGs.[8]

---

8. Diagnosis-related groups (DRGs) is a system used in the United States to classify hospital cases, with the intent to identify the "products" that a hospital provides. DRGs are used to determine how much Medicare pays the hospital for each "product," with the reasoning that patients within each category are clinically similar and are expected to use the same level of hospital resources.

At the time (early in healthcare reform), inpatient nursing was heavily resistant to any financially driven change, and so the whole situation presented a difficult political and cultural challenge to the organization.

APPROACH

An endeavor to resolve the issues was complex. No single process could be tackled in isolation from the others, and so this was a classic example of a Tier 3 program (as introduced in Chapter 2), where each concept for multiple-component processes had to be designed and agreed upon in tandem, prior to any detailed design and implementation.

Figure 4.7 shows the primary processes and concepts that were redesigned. Given the political sensitivity and the sheer complexity of the endeavor, the project was co-led by a seasoned, highly respected internal (RN) Black Belt and the author as an external MBB.

Once the concepts were developed, a multifaceted implementation plan ensued, as shown in Figure 4.8. The MBB played the primary lead for the concept design work, while the Black Belt was the primary lead for the more significant volume of implementation work.

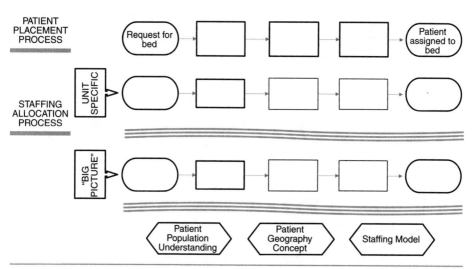

Figure 4.7 Major processes and models redesigned during the project

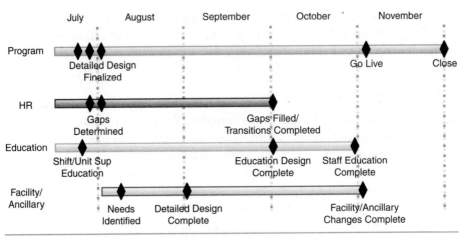

Figure 4.8 Inpatient Placement implementation plan

CHANGES MADE

The most significant changes made in the project were first, how patients were grouped and where they were placed geographically (which units did what), and second, how the units were staffed in terms of their basic operating models. Based on these changes, one whole inpatient unit became a flex unit and closed during low census, only to open during peak demands.

Three major processes were also streamlined and had clear accountabilities set: the patient placement process, long-term staffing (staff budgeting, forecasting, and scheduling), and short-term staffing (flexing to demand).

RESULTS

The flexing of units affected unit utilization substantially, taking it from 55% to more than 80%. The impact of this, along with the changes to staff planning and flexing, generated staffing savings of more than $600,000 per year.

LEADERSHIP LEARNING

Leadership learning from this project includes the following:

1. Some projects are well beyond a simple structure and have to be tackled as a fairly complex (Tier 3) program. The interconnectedness of the processes meant that they had to be redesigned together, rather than sequentially.

2. For politically or culturally sensitive projects, the use of seasoned and credible Project Leader(s) is crucial.

3. At the time, this type of project had never been conducted within any of the benchmark organizations contacted. Sometimes it's important just to go ahead and cut new ground.

4. In such a complex process set there needed to be many Champions—the whole Executive Team in this case. To ensure that they moved forward together, all had to (literally) sign off on the concept.

EPILOGUE

This same successful project approach has since been repeated a number of times, for example, within a major healthcare system in a different state and also again in this same hospital to move to single-occupancy rooms.

CASE 12: NEW EMERGENCY DEPARTMENT DESIGN

BACKGROUND/SITUATION

A health system had struggled with a suboptimal footprint and layout of its ED in its main hospital for many years. The ED had been designed for fewer than 20,000 patients per year, but it was now seeing more than double that volume.

Leadership had opted to build a whole new ED rather than revamp the existing one. Initial schematics had been created, but concerns over designing the new ED with inherent process and flow weaknesses drove the ED leadership team to back up and commit time and effort prior to the architectural design to consider the process aspects of the new space in an effort to "build in leanness."

APPROACH

Prior to the final schematic design phase, three additional phases were conducted, all led by Lean Sigma resources:

1. Voice of the Customer

2. ED process requirements analysis, to examine and understand core processes both within the ED, as well as those connecting the ED to ancillary areas

3. Layout concept design, taking into consideration output from the first two phases

Once the detailed schematics were finalized, multiple standardization events tackled the core ED processes to ensure that they were well integrated and took maximum advantage of the new layout.

CHANGES MADE

Based on the work, a number of changes were made to the original designs, including the following:

- External perimeter changes to ensure close proximity of the main entrance to greeters
- The addition of rapid medical examination (RME) rooms in a suite of rapid access rooms close to the entrance
- Locating support rooms away from the main ED space to create a more compact environment
- Designing multiple hub spaces (nursing stations) instead of just one to bring staff closer to all treatment rooms (and thus patients)

RESULTS

At the time of writing the construction has commenced for the new ED. The design received an overwhelming positive response from all audiences from the community to the Board of Trustees to the frontline staff.

LEADERSHIP LEARNING

Leadership learning from this project includes the following:

1. Lean Sigma process and flow considerations were combined into the more traditional design and build process.
2. Lean Sigma resources were used to lead, alongside architects and construction.
3. It's best to get the design right the first time, instead of redesigning or compromising later.
4. Include VOC to ensure that nothing was missed.
5. Take advantage to advertise and brand the approach, to gain awareness and credibility in the community.

COMMENCING THE JOURNEY

5

Most organizations tend to follow a similar early path on the Lean Sigma journey, starting with a low-resource, low-commitment "testing of the waters." Typically this takes the form of one or two interested operations leaders identifying an individual or small handful of resources to attend a locally offered training, either at another nearby healthcare organization, through their third-party provider, or through a local academic institution. The selected individuals attempt a project on a very part-time basis and achieve reasonable, but limited, success.

The activity can remain in this state almost indefinitely if no further investment of effort is made on the part of leadership. Small, local-level project success will aid the sponsoring leaders, but no breakthrough in organizational performance will ensue until the broader Executive Team recognizes the value and is willing to grow the initial endeavor into something more—a program of some sort.

The stages of maturity, including this initial Level 0, are shown in Table 5.1.

Many leaders mistakenly believe they are beyond this early exploration but wonder why they aren't getting the real traction they are seeking, when in reality they may have some facets of a mature program in place but are missing some of the more basic program elements.

The key step here is deliberateness: taking time as an Executive Team to decide on the purpose and appropriate structure for a program—program design. All levels of an organization's structure (executive, leadership, and

Table 5.1   Stages of Lean Sigma Program Maturity in Healthcare

	Early Exploration (Level 0)	Launch (Level 1)	Critical Mass (Level 2)	Scale Replication (Level 3)	Institutionalization (Level 4)
Leadership	1–2 visionaries	Core of Exec Team	Majority of Exec Team Key directors	Exec Team Majority of directors	Expected for all leaders
People	Driven few	Early adopters Most still skeptical	Early majority Many still skeptical	Late majority Few still skeptical	Career path
Project Leaders	Small group of "testers"	Initial select few, full time Small cadre part time	Centralized core of full time Supporting team of part time	Core full-time team plus few decentralized Large mass of trained leaders to draw upon	Core full-time team plus many decentralized Large mass of trained leaders to draw upon
Scope	Single department or process	Few core operations departments	Majority of core operations departments Few non-core departments	Expected for core internal areas Extended to supporting non-core plus external	Expected for whole organization
Infrastructure	None	Established but limited Initial program thinking	Centralized robust program	Centralized robust program Additional decentralized support structure	Centralized strategic program remains Embedded MBBs in major business units

Training	External public training (YB, GB)	On-site Executive, Champion Focused GB, BB training Led by external resource	Waves of Champion, GB, BB training Led by external resource BBs lead internal awareness sessions	Waves of Champion GB, BB training Led by external resource BBs take on more training, coaching activity	Majority led by internal MBB Select training by external resource Built into new hire training
Projects	Initial test projects, based on pain	Burning platform Initial project hopper	Low-hanging fruit Key strategic projects Established project pipeline	Driven by strategy Pilot and proliferate More complex tiers Process design	Key mechanism to deliver strategy Portfolio view
Impact	Limited but useful results	Primarily cost reduction	Strong cost reduction focus Additional quality and service projects	Across all pillars Tied to leader evaluation	Tied to staff evaluation The way we improve
Tracking/ Reporting	None	Defined financial tracking Initial sharing of success	All projects tracked for financials Formal communication plan in place	Broad communication of results	Built into operational planning and reports

management) need to be involved in order to build a successful change program, but this shouldn't be done in an arbitrary fashion. Careful deployment design and execution are critical. Figure 5.1 shows a simple phased deployment approach. The approach is cyclical (for reasons to be explained later) and commences with the senior Executive Team.

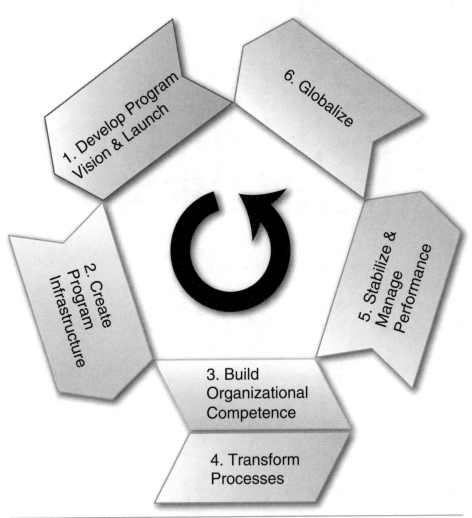

Figure 5.1 Model for performance improvement deployment

I. PROGRAM VISION AND LAUNCH

Creating the foundation for a successful, integrated deployment begins with the Executive Team reaching consensus on what they want to achieve from the program and how they envision its structure—more specifically, to finalize and agree on the program concept, roles and responsibilities, timeline, resource selection and commitments, business case, and initial projects.

To achieve this, the key leadership and stakeholders are convened to define the collective vision for the program. To create this common vision, the Executive Team considers (in order) the following:

- What are the desired outcomes from the program (perhaps cultural, results, strategy execution, etc.)?

- What are the likely business problems to which the program will be applied? For example, growth, cost savings, quality, etc.

- What past/current initiatives have been undertaken? What were their successes and shortfalls? How will this program fit with those initiatives? For example, one particular program needed to connect directly with the organizational goal of performance excellence. Rather than create a new endeavor, the existing fragmented activity was unified, retasked, and realigned with the new approaches.

- How will the program fit with the current business model? Will it be centralized for the health system (say) or decentralized across it? Where will the accountability for program results lie?

- What are the preferred improvement methodologies (Lean, Six Sigma, other)? Are there any that must be avoided or downplayed?

- Who are the proposed Project Leaders? What are their time commitments, distribution, and depth of expertise? For one particular system it was decided that five leaders would be trained to a Black Belt level and float across three hospitals, tackling projects where they were most needed, rather than being dedicated to any one particular site.

- What is the likely scope of the deployment (operations, clinical processes, business, growth, supply chain, etc.)? For example, prior to a broader program being undertaken, one Executive Team chose to commence the program on a smaller scale in three of its system hospitals and to focus just on nursing. This allowed a more controlled beginning, a simpler initial focus of resources, demonstration of concept, and a learning environment for how this might work in the organization.

- Are there any preferred initial steps to move forward, such as process improvement or process standardization?
- What are the infrastructure requirements to support the program? What is the magnitude? Are they centralized or decentralized?
- What are the expectations for execution and delivering results? When should the program break even? How much return on investment (ROI) is being sought?
- What is the plan for internalization of mentoring and training skills?
- What are the constraints or barriers to being successful in the program?
- What is the ongoing role of any consulting partner(s)? For how long is consulting support needed?

Based on the answers to these questions, the Executive Team can agree on the program concept, roles and responsibilities, timeline, resource selection and commitments, and the business case and identify some initial projects.

II. CREATING PROGRAM INFRASTRUCTURE

Infrastructure is effectively the difference between just running a project here and there and having a fully functioning long-term program. Certain key elements need to be in place to ensure that the program has a robust foundation:

- **An active Steering Group:** To ensure ongoing focus and emphasize organizational commitment to the program, a Steering Group should be formed, meeting at least monthly to guide the program and ensure that key decisions are made and executed.
- **Human resources engagement:** The role of a number of individuals will change; therefore it will be necessary to involve HR to make active consideration of the associated organizational aspects. These include criteria for personnel selection, reward and recognition, career path planning, succession, and responsibility shifting and evaluation.
- **Mechanisms to track projects and financial returns:** To ensure that the program is successful in bringing value to the organization, it is important to ensure that financial returns are measured consistently using business rules, with specific guidelines on how and what to measure. In addition, the program may benefit from a project database that tracks the progress

of individual projects as well as across the portfolio. This can range from a database software acquisition for a larger organization to a simple spreadsheet.

- **An initial Communication Plan and package (reporting, messaging, and timing for the relevant audiences):** In order to ensure the long-term viability of the program, acceptance by key leaders across the enterprise is important. A Communication Plan should ensure that stakeholders receive a consistent message, including how the program fits with corporate strategies and operations, roles, accountability, time frame, and goals.

- **An inventory of potential projects, ready for implementation when the program is launched.**

- **Finalized project selection and draft Charters for the initial training wave of projects.** A project needs to be simple enough for the novice leader to complete in reasonable time but bring significant business value to the organization.

- **Finalized event selection and draft Charters for any initial quick-win Kaizen events.**

III. DEVELOPING ORGANIZATIONAL COMPETENCE

Changing a healthcare organization at the process level is very much about changing the people, both in behaviors and in performance, but also in competencies. To address persistent, stubborn business problems, proficiencies are necessary that are perhaps insufficiently available within the organization.

Competency development is usually thought to be synonymous with training, and as such training is often made the first priority without due consideration and planning. Unfortunately, classes are thus misaligned with the real competency development needs.

Building competency takes some thought to effectively and efficiently train the right people with the right skills. Following a plan of identifying needs and assessing current capabilities allows the Steering Group to develop just the talent needed, with a much greater level of success.

Figure 5.2 shows the basic flow underpinning competency development. As described previously, before jumping into training classes, earlier considerations need to be made. Within the adult training environment, classes need to deliver on the different skill sets, from executive-level awareness to the Project Leaders to the frontline staff. Exactly whom should we be training and on what? A little

Figure 5.2 The flow of competency development

planning and thought are required. Thus, working backward in Figure 5.2 from the training itself:

- Before commencing training, the **training structure and approach** need to be defined and the materials generated to ensure that the classes will achieve the desired results.
- The classes are there to bridge a gap in knowledge, and so the **gaps** themselves must be understood. These are the major **educational requirements** for each role, that is, who needs to be taught what?
- To understand the gaps, the desired **skills** must be understood. What exactly do the trainees need to know?
- The desired skills are based on the **methods** we want them to employ and the **roadmaps** we want them to follow.
- The methods and roadmaps we want them to follow depend heavily on the **roles** we expect those individuals to play and within what defined **organization structure.** Are we looking to create a cadre of highly skilled change resources, crack commandos if you like, or an army of foot soldiers? The roles determine the skill levels required.
- The final step, working backward from training, is that the roles we want these individuals to play are based primarily on the **business need** we have at hand.

Thus, if we want to train the right people with the right skills in the most efficient and effective manner possible, we need to understand exactly what we are trying to achieve, what types of business problems we are trying to solve, and thus how best to structure our change resources.

In the vast majority of cases, organizations choose to build an internal capacity to deliver change, a cadre of autonomous change agents capable of applying the methodologies and tools to create value on an ongoing basis. These individuals may be that smaller, centralized corps of highly skilled specialists assigned to broader problem resolution, or they may be a larger, perhaps lower-skilled group dispersed throughout the organization to address local issues. These questions need to be asked early, with the understanding that the solution may be a mix of these.

It is important to school not only the change leaders in the right approaches, but also the recipients of change, along with other key stakeholders. Potentially the whole complement of staff may need to be engaged and given the appropriate skills and abilities to function as change is introduced, to realize the strongest impact and sustained results. Training needs, then, should be characterized as follows:

- To ensure that all projects in the program are successful, each project will have an internal Champion assigned to support the Project Leader (Black or Green Belt). The Champions will need to receive training outlining their various roles and interactions, and how they should be reviewing and supporting the projects, to ensure that barriers are identified and mitigated or removed.

- The Process Owner and recipients of change are trained and mentored to strengthen accountability and thus ensure sustained ongoing performance.

- The Steering Group is guided and mentored to finalize the infrastructure, identify and select the next project and Belt opportunities, ensure that the desired business value is achieved, and identify problems or issues and make course corrections if needed.

With respect to the training itself, classroom training is not the only vehicle for developing competencies. Each Project Leader is assigned a project to lead under the guidance of a seasoned project mentor, to ensure that they understand the right tools to use, in what order, along with the correct technical application. In addition, participation in projects facilitated by seasoned external resources, as a Team member or even as an observer, provides an opportunity to witness, close up, how the methodology and tools, learned in theory, are applied in practice. Both approaches accelerate the Belt's ability to consistently bring project results autonomously and provide a dramatic difference in the return on investment.

E-learning is often a good supporting tool to create awareness of the program more broadly across the organization and is useful as a reference tool for practitioners once initial, more hands-on training is complete.

IV. TRANSFORMING PROCESSES

Aside from the inherent advantage in delivering improvements, successful projects, especially in the early stages, bring visibility to the program, provide the training ground for Project Leaders, and provide the financial and cultural capital to fuel the program. This early concentration of effort provides an excellent opportunity to communicate proof of the program concept to the rest of the organization.

By pursuing projects meaningful to the organization, leaders learn the value the program provides to the organization, how it works, their role within it, the associated benefit, and the importance as a business change methodology. Projects may be identified, either driven by the strategic or annual operating plans or well recognized as "points of pain." A full organizational assessment is usually not necessary for initial project selection, since leaders typically have insight into problem areas and processes that require prompt attention.

The Steering Group and Champions identify, prioritize, and sequence projects, balancing the need for projects to develop new Project Leaders with the business need for results; assigning some projects to leaders in training, others to existing change agents within the organization, and still others, when appropriate, to external resources.

A spread of projects is key, in that it allows for the management of resources to not overburden one department or area but also brings some diversity in the types of returns gained. In the early stages especially, it's important that the program not be perceived as singularly focused, as "just a quality thing" or "just a finance thing." Some suggestions for considering these other types of returns are shown in Table 5.2.

The Steering Committee may also identify mission-critical or politically sensitive projects that cannot await internal training, or there may be complex interdepartmental projects that require prompt attention. In such cases, these projects that would be difficult for a novice internal change leader earlier in the deployment could be more appropriately led by skilled, experienced external resources.

To create support for the program and to gain some quick initial returns on investment, Kaizen events are often utilized. These events might provisionally target key finance processes such as billing with the goal of potentially funding the program for the charter year. The events are typically conducted in the first six to eight weeks of the program.

Table 5.2 Example Projects by Driver and Type

Driver	Project Types	Examples
Quality and Safety	CMS measure optimization	Incidents of falls, pressure ulcers, or CAUTI
	Improved patient flow	Door to balloon time
Service	Reduced lengths of stay and wait times	ED length of stay
	Improved patient flow	Registration throughput and flow
Profitability	Reduced costs	Reducing supply costs
		Balancing staffing with demand
	Improved flow of cash	Billing timeliness and accuracy
		Reducing A/R
Growth	Increased capacity	Ramping up new services
	Improved revenue capture	Charge capture
		Increasing reimbursement
		Reducing late charges
People	Reduced waste and inefficiency	Any process with low employee engagement scores

V. Stabilization and Performance Management

The most critical component of operational improvement is the Control Plan. Without that, even the best-intentioned improvements tend to drift back to the old way of doing things. Once improvements are made, process by process, robust Control Plans are put in place to ensure that performance is managed and sustained. As described in Chapter 3, the Control Plan for a process focuses on the decision making within and around the process to ensure clear accountability for responding to impending performance change, in a standardized way, and to mitigate problems appropriately.

In support of this control, the Process Owner and recipients of change receive training and mentoring in process standardization methods and performance management. Part of managing change is to know when to change and when not to change. Leaders learn not to overreact and instigate unneeded change. By resisting unwarranted change, the leader brings a calm to work processes and reduces the resource drain of persistent tweaking.

Leaders may opt to more rapidly bring about this process stabilization, rather than waiting for the application of change projects, by conducting sequences of multiple individual standardization events, as described in Chapter 3.[1] Even though this isn't a change approach, significant improvements in performance arise in more than half of processes.

In addition to performance management for processes, the overall program begins to settle into a rhythm in this phase. Ongoing Steering Group meetings continue to identify new opportunities, ensure that the business value is achieved (with reports to the executive on project and training status as well as returns), and to recognize and make needed course corrections. The future of the program depends on continuous oversight and the constant communication of successes.

VI. GLOBALIZATION

A vast majority of programs commence with a focused start in one area of the business—a service line, perhaps, or within a few core functions. Clearly, benefits are achievable across the whole organization, so once the program is performing well and stabilized, it can be extended to other parts of the business. This in itself takes careful planning to avoid any misfires. Many programs run aground due to leaders underestimating the difficulties of extending to new areas. In most instances, it's usually best to approach this with the same level of planning detail as the original focus.

Sometimes extension to new areas requires different approaches, such as new service development techniques or process design, which require some different management approaches and competences. As much as the DMAIC roadmap is a wonderfully flexible approach, it isn't the one size that fits all.

PHASE I REVISITED

The cyclical nature of Figure 5.1 is an important aspect of these approaches. The initial vision and focus developed in the first cycle were based on a multitude of both internal and external factors, including, but not limited to,

- Relative market position
- Cost structure and financial performance
- Propensity for change

---

1. Examples of such events as applied to registration and admission processes are described in Chapter 4.

- Capacity of key processes
- Quality and service indicators, etc.

After many change projects have been conducted on what were key business problems, ideally many of these factors have been impacted and the landscape has changed. Just the simple fact that now the organization has more advanced capability for change can impact how the program is viewed.

It is extremely common for healthcare organizations to focus their Lean Sigma program on cost reduction in the first two years. This should be an extremely successful approach, but leaders quickly realize they can't save their way to prosperity, and so a course adjustment is needed. Rather than do this in an arbitrary way, starting at the vision phase again pays dividends.

Second cycles can vary but often focus on growth, stabilization, or even extension beyond the realm of the initial organization—for example, moving from a single hospital to a system or perhaps extending to adjacent providers in the supply chain. In all of these cases it's important to revisit the vision and ensure that the supporting infrastructure and competencies are in place.

HOW TO START

The hardest part of any journey is often taking the first step. My strongest advice, therefore, regarding starting is that you actually should start.[2]

Now.

As mentioned earlier in this chapter, many organizations arguably have started the journey, or are in that Level 0, but stepping up to Level 1 requires energy to overcome the inertia. Leaders don't typically drift into this; it requires a spark. Many leaders understand the value, but it still requires that catalyst.

A useful activity is to consider your organization's readiness to deploy. Who is already "there"? Are there any key leverage leaders to make this happen?

It's important to solicit support, but don't hand this off. Ask key individuals to read this book, or parts of it that you think will resonate with them. Talk to, or better still visit, organizations that already have done well with Lean Sigma. If you don't know any, take a look at the acknowledgments section of this book.

Above all, someone, wherever he or she is in the business, needs to drive this.

Why not you?

Why not now?

---

2. In the words of Walt Disney, "The way to get started is to quit talking and begin doing."

INDEX